Songs from the Magical Tradition

by
Jerry Bird

GREEN
MAGIC

Songs from the Magical Tradition © 2012 by Jerry Bird. All rights reserved. No part of this book may be used or reproduced in any form without written permission of the author, except in the case of quotations in articles and reviews.

Green Magic
5 Stathe Cottages
Stathe
Somerset
TA7 0JL
England

www.greenmagicpublishing.com
info@greenmagicpublishing.com

Cover image by Jerry Bird
(sculpture by Tach Pollard)

Typeset by Green Man Books, Dorchester
www.greenmanbooks.co.uk

ISBN 978-0-9566197-0-9

GREEN MAGIC

> This book is dedicated to the memory of
> Maria Cunningham
> 1958 - 2012

Jerry Bird is a professional writer and musician living in Dorset. He has edited, and been the major contributor to, *Merry Meet Magazine,* a quarterly journal of 'folklore and pagan heritage', since its inception in 1999. He has also contributed articles to other publications such as *Quest, The Cauldron, Pagan Dawn,* and *English Dance and Song.*

He is passionate about folk music and currently plays fiddle, guitar and mandolin with the folk-rock band 'State of Undress', as well as performing solo, and occasionally with Dorset's young folksinging prodigy, James Findlay.

The author (right) with James Findlay (photo: Alastair Simpson)

Other books by Jerry Bird published by Green Magic:
Landscape of Memory (2009)
Ancient Stones on Old Postcards (2011)

The author acknowledges the scholarship and expertise of all the writers whose works he has consulted, especially Bob Stewart, whose *Where is Saint George?* (1977) was an important source of inspiration. Another was the compilation CD *Songs of Witchcraft and Magic* (2007), with extensive sleeve notes by Joyce Froome, produced by the Museum of Witchcraft in Boscastle, who also kindly allowed me access to their extensive library.

Thanks are due to my wife Diane, for her constructive criticism of some of the essays included here, and to my parents for the gift of the 1957 edition of Child's *English and Scottish Ballads*. Laurence Keen OBE, archaeological consultant to *Merry Meet Magazine*, once again kindly read my proofs, and also provided the illustration on page 16 (©Keen) from his extensive collection of material on medieval floor-tiles.

The songs are, of course, all in the public domain, except for the marvellous reconstruction of the ballad of 'Childe Rowland' (pages 129-131) which was created by Maria Cunningham, who sadly died just before the publication of this book. The arrangements are all my own, apart from the above mentioned, along with 'Tam Lin' and 'Lady Margaret', the melodies for which I have transcribed from the singing of James Findlay, my great friend and occasional musical collaborator, who also provided the photograph of the Symonds cider apple wassail on page 93.

The Mudcat Cafe internet site has been invaluable in suggesting source material, and much use has been made of the increasingly comprehensive library of out-of-print works available on internet sites such as www.gutenberg.org and www.sacred-texts.com. The EFDSS website also now displays a wealth of archive material. Several illustrations have been sourced from www.fromoldbooks.com, with its extensive collection of royalty-free stock images (pages 2, 6, 9, 33, 118, 137). The engraving on page 29 is from Pete Gotto's collection, and that on page 60 from Sue Leadley's. Other images are from the author's own collection and/or are otherwise in the public domain.

Contents

	Dedication	ii
	Acknowledgements	iii
	Preface	v
	Introduction	vii
1.	The Astrologer	1
2.	The Bells of Paradise	7
3.	The Boar's Head Carol	11
4.	Childe Rowland	21
5.	Clerk Colvill	31
6.	The Cutty Wren	37
7.	Hal-An-Tow	43
8.	Jennifer Gentle	51
9.	John Barleycorn	57
10.	King Orfeo	63
11.	Lady Margaret	71
12.	The Lambton Worm	77
13.	The Somerset Wassail	83
14.	Tam Lin	95
15.	Thomas The Rhymer	105
16.	The Two Magicians	113
17.	Widdecombe Fair	119
	MUSIC	127
	Bibliography	147
	Index	149

Preface

This book is partly written with a Pagan readership in mind, for whom the relevance of traditional folk music to modern Paganism may hitherto not have been immediately apparent. For example some songs, such as 'John Barleycorn' and the 'Hal-An-Tow' song, are intimately connected with the cycle of the seasons, and cry out for inclusion in, in these two cases, Lammas and Beltane celebrations. Others, such as the 'Two Magicians' and the 'Cutty Wren', with their strong chorus lines, would be excellent for raising energy in a circle, while some of the longer, more mysterious ballads, such as 'Tam Lin' or 'Childe Rowland' would be very suitable for guided meditations or 'pathworkings'.

Songs from the Magical Tradition is also, of course, aimed at anyone who enjoys folk music, and wishes to explore the background of some of its more intriguing aspects. Many previous studies have been written in a somewhat dry, academic way, as if aimed at impressing other experts rather than promoting the enjoyment of the subject to a wider audience. I hope I have achieved my aim of producing a study that is accessible to a more general readership without diluting its serious content.

Last, but certainly not least, the book is a resource for musicians and singers, and to that end musical notation with chords has been included. For some of the songs, alternative versions are given, usually where the lyrics, as scrutinized in the text, differ from the way in which they are now commonly performed.

The songs in this anthology are from a variety of sources, and these are mentioned in the text. The musical arrangements, which are based on traditional settings, are my own, except for 'Tam Lin' and 'Lady Margaret', which have been transcribed from the singing of James Findlay, and Maria Cunningham's reconstruction of 'Childe Rowland'. I have tried to present the music in as user-friendly a manner as possible by transposing the melodies, where necessary, into keys suitable for the most popular folk instruments — fiddle, mandolin, guitar, etc. For good measure, a few relevant instrumental tunes have also been included, and these are presented in the keys in which they are most usually played in pub sessions and folk clubs.

This is a relatively small selection of songs, compared with the *genre* as a whole, and readers interested in exploring the subject futher are recommended to consult many of the sources listed in the bibliography at the end of the book. Of these, certainly the most important is Child's *English and Scottish Ballads*, which while now very expensive to buy, is thankfully available online. A wealth of material is also available on the website, and from the online bookshop of, the English Folk Dance and Song Society (EFDSS).

While researching material for this book, I came across my long-lost, battered and dog-eared copy of *English, Welsh, Scottish & Irish Fiddle Tunes* (see next page), and for the first time I looked at the 'Relevant Material' section inside the back cover. I was amused and delighted to find, among the titles listed, Robert Graves' *The White Goddess*, Margaret Murray's *The God of the Witches*, and Lewis Spence's *Magic Arts in Celtic Britain*. The wheel had turned full circle — I had reconnected with the magical tradition.

Introduction

I must have been about sixteen when Tom Williamson, my violin tutor, suggested that I should try playing some traditional folk tunes, as light relief from the Associated Examination Board violin syllabus pieces, of which I was becoming weary. A visit to Duck, Son and Pinker, the late lamented music emporium next to Bath's famous Pultney Bridge, furnished me with a copy of Robin Williamson's then newly-published *English, Welsh, Scottish & Irish Fiddle Tunes*. In hindsight it has been one of the most important books I have ever owned: I fell instantly in love with those quirky, often beautiful tunes with their insistent rhythms, unusual modality and intricate decoration. About the same time I heard, for the first time, June Tabor's stunning *Ashes and Diamonds* album, played in its entirety on the radio by the legendary John Peel, and I was delighted to find she was performing locally in the Hat and Feather folk club in Walcot Street — more delighted still when I found myself able to attend without being quizzed about my age.

Later, at university, I spent a lot of time busking in the subways of Birmingham, spending a large proportion of the proceeds at Reddington's Rare Records, opposite Moor Street Station, buying early Fairport Convention, Incredible String Band and Carthy-Swarbrick albums, and playing in various pubs and folk clubs, including the Grey Cock folk club where I was privileged to see Charles Parker, Ewan McColl and Peggy Seeger perform.

Back in Bath there was a thriving folk music scene in the early eighties, and among the regulars on the 'Celtic music' circuit was a quietly spoken long-haired chap called Bob Stewart, who would bring a replica medieval cittern, or sometimes a psaltery to the Bathwick Arms sessions; there I also met Marko, Neil and Forbes, the lads with whom I often played at 'Yon Canny Band' gigs.

I had always been vaguely aware of a mystical strand that ran through the British folk music tradition, from the Yeatsian 'Celtic mist' that infused the work of many Irish bands such as Clannad and Planxty, to the arcane weirdness of the English morris tradition as explored by Ashley Hutchings *et al* in the *Morris On* recordings. Ironically it was only after moving to Sussex many years later, and becoming immersed in the latter tradition, that I discovered Bob Stewart's seminal work on pagan imagery in English folk song *Where Is Saint George?* (1977), having been asked for copies many times at my Green Man Bookshop in Eastbourne; it had been published around the time I was first sneaking into the Hat and Feather folk club all those years before.

Bob Stewart's book is a wonderful compendium of musical erudition and esoteric lore, linking together Druidic teachings, the Hebrew Qabbalah, Christian mysticism, and tarot cards, among other things. His thesis, briefly, is that elements of a pre-Christian, 'western mystery tradition' entered the folk tradition long ago, and that a lot of the imagery, along with certain musical phrases, found in folk songs, are common to Celtic and pre-Celtic worship; some of this had survived suppression by, and was even absorbed by the Christian Church. Robert Graves, in *The White Goddess: a Historical Grammar of Poetic Myth* (1948), espouses similar opinions, though in his case he seems to have become fixated by the idea of an ancient Goddess-based religion which survived by becoming subsumed in a 'witch-cult', which preserved ancient pagan lore and religion — a hypothesis first proposed by Margaret Murray in *The Witch Cult in Western Europe* (1921), and expanded in *The God of the Witches* (1931). To Graves the best British ballads contained the essence of the 'Old Religion', and their 'language of poetic myth', represented 'a magical language bound up with popular religious ceremonies in honour of the Moon-goddess'.

Where is Saint George? and *The White Goddess* are both important books, and the latter has been very influential in the development of modern Paganism, especially Wicca, despite (or maybe even partly because of) its lack of scholarly rigour. Graves has often been accused of starting with a thesis and then being highly selective in his use of material in order to justify his argument, a criticism also levelled (with perhaps even more justification) against Margaret Murray. Ronald Hutton, writing about the *The White Goddess* states that it 'remains a major source of confusion about the ancient Celts and influences many un-scholarly views of Celtic paganism'. Perhaps because of this, what I have called the 'magical tradition' seems to have become somewhat sidelined in more recent studies, and has not since been treated seriously as a *genre* in its own right. The songs collected here are usually anthologized in various other categories, often with just a cursory mention that they contain some element of the supernatural in their narrative.

This book makes no particular assertions, other than the fact that there is a very strong element of supernatural magic contained within a substantial part of the British folk song tradition; it presents a representative anthology of some relevant songs, in alphabetical order, along with extensive notes on their historical context, imagery, and possible origins. In these, I have deliberately shied away from drawing any firm conclusions, and the reader is left to decide for themselves how relevant the songs might be in the wider contexts of historical and contemporary paganism and magic. In a sense, therefore, the book is a little like a journey with no destination, but very often on journeys, travelling is more important than arriving, and the author hopes you will very much enjoy this guided exploration of the magical tradition.

music page 128

1. The Astrologer

It's of a bold astrologer in London town did dwell,
At telling maidens' fortunes, there's none could him excel,
There was a nice young serving girl a-living there close by,
She came one day to the astrologer all for to have a try.

"I hear that you tell fortunes, sir, would you tell me mine?" said she,
"Of course, my dear, without a doubt if you'll walk upstairs with me."
"To walk upstairs with you, kind sir, I'm sure I am afraid,"
She spoke it in such modesty as though she were a maid.

"To walk upstairs with me, my dear, you need not be afraid,
Knowing it was but the other day you with your master laid"
Then she began to curse and swear she would her master bring,
As witness for both him and her that it was no such thing.

"My pretty maid, don't swear and curse, you'll make the deed the worse,
For the crown piece that he gave to you, you've got it in your purse"
"Oh! indeed you can tell fortunes, sir, you've told me mine," said she,
And out she pulled the crown piece —"Good morning, sir, said she.

This song was collected by Henry Hammond and George Gardiner from a Mr J. Penny, and Marina Russell in Dorset in 1906 and 1907, and is published in the collection *Marrow Bones*. It tells one of the oldest stories in the world — that of a glamorous charlatan's attempt to woo a young lady, on this occasion using his supposed skills as an astrologer. The twist in the tale is that the astrologer, who is portrayed as a predatory womanizer, does indeed have some magical skills in divination, and the maid, who is not nearly as innocent nor demure as she makes out, finds herself well and truly caught out.

Since Elizabethan times, at least, the social standing of conjurors and astrologers had a lot in common with musicians. As a class they were considered to be little more than vagrants, often travellers to boot, going where the work was, and frequently combining their profession with other occupations. Both were also at times reviled by the Church, though some clergy were apt, occasionally, to dabble in astrological matters. However, the very lucky, and/or the highly skilled, in either profession, might sometimes become the liveried staff of wealthy households or even royalty, ending up comfortably off with a house, land and a pension in their dotage, though the political favours and fortunes of their patrons could make such a living precarious in the extreme. Even luminaries in their field such as Nostrodamus, astrologer to the Court of the Medicis, eventually fell foul of accusations of witchcraft; Doctor John Dee was famously astrologer to Queen Elizabeth I, but ended up dying in poverty after a series of misfortunes, and after the mercurial anti-occultist James I had refused to support him.

The common perception of the cunning man or woman in early modern times is that of the solitary practitioner, living alone or perhaps with a familiar, on the edge of a village practising herbal medicine, fortune-telling, midwifery and selling spells and charms to ward off evil spirits and witchcraft. However, the belief in magic did not die with the migration of the working population to towns and cities in the industrial revolution, even though the breakdown of close-knit rural communities led to a gradual reduction in accusations of witchcraft — often the stock-in-trade of the magical practitioner: many cunning folk would have migrated to where their work was to be found. London, particularly, was a magnet for large numbers of fortune-tellers and magicians from medieval times onwards, some of whom used it as a base for commercial tours of surrounding country towns and villages. True magicians and cunning folk generally considered themselves rather a cut-above-the common fortune-tellers, many of whom were traditionally of gypsy origin, but they nevertheless competed in the same market.

The Book of Spirits, **from Francis Barrett's** *Magus* **(1801)**

Indeed, the proliferation of fortune-tellers was viewed with some alarm by those who regarded astrology as a genuine science — a worthy pursuit for the intellectual mind. In the first half of the nineteenth century a society of fortune-tellers was formed called the Mercurii of London, who sought to raise the standard of astrological prediction. Two of the principal astrologers associated with this society were Robert Cross Smith (1795-1832), who wrote under the pen-name 'Raphael', and Richard James Morrison (1795 -1874), who wrote as 'Zadkiel'. They promoted the work of the eighteenth-century doctor and astrologer Ebenezer Sibley, and their 1825 *Compendium of Astrology, Geomancy and Occult Philosophy* which many regard as a classic of its kind helped to kick-start a revival of serious interest in the subject that still continues; *Raphael's Ephemeris* remains popular to this day.

Songs from the Magical Tradition

The Astrologer, from Hans Holbein's *Dance of Death* (1538)

Even in the nineteenth and twentieth centuries, fortune-tellers operated on the outer fringes of legality. The Vagrancy Act of 1824 outlawed 'persons pretending or professing to tell fortunes, or using any subtle craft, means and device, by palmistry or otherwise, to deceive and impose'. This, and continuing prosecutions under the Witchcraft Act of 1732 threatened the profession of the cunning folk, although the establishment of official county police forces in 1851 did pretty much eradicate the 'witch mobbings' of previous years. However, it appears that the law was not rigorously enforced, except where it was blatantly flouted by the over-promotion of a fortune-teller's skills, for example, or in the case of practitioners who were denounced to police or magistrates by dissatisfied or overcharged customers. During this period many astrologers advertized openly in newspapers, even those whose editorial stance was firmly against popular superstition. An Occultist's Defence League was founded in the 1890s and eventually prosecutions began to wane, culminating in the abolition of both acts after the notorious trial of the psychic Helen Duncan in 1951.

The song probably dates from the mid nineteenth century and gives an intriguing snapshot of the Victorian underclass in

The Astrologer

London at a time when divination was proving very popular, especially among the female half of the population, and a thriving army of cunning men and women made a living exploiting the superstition of many. This was a period when magical grimoires, almanacs and divination manuals and magazines were becoming widely available in cheap editions, due largely to the new development of large scale wood-pulp paper-mills. Thomas Hardy's character Tess Durbeyfield hides a well-thumbed copy of *The Compleat Fortune Teller* in the thatch of an outhouse to assuage her mother's 'curious fetichistic fear' of it when it is not actually being consulted.

With divination, there has always been a tendency to place more trust in the message than the messenger. Even today, if you say you have consulted a palmist, tarot reader, or crystal-gazer the reaction will often be ridicule, but tinged with a real desire to know the outcome. In this sense, modern-day psychics, healers, tarotists or rune-readers are generally no more trusted than the cunning folk of old, yet people still flock to them in droves, especially at psychic fairs and the like.

The song exploits this paradox neatly. We have what, at first, appears to be a gullible young serving girl seeking to have her fortune told by a renowned London astrologer, only to be asked to 'walk upstairs' with the gentleman. Playing the innocent maid she pretends to be shocked and refuses, only to be caught out by the man with a home truth — that she has recently lain with her master. When she denies the charge, swearing and cursing the man, he hits back that she herself is carrying the proof of this allegation in her purse. The girl finally admits that the astrologer does indeed have magical abilities 'Oh! indeed you can tell fortunes, sir' adding 'you've told me mine' — perhaps even a tacit acknowledgment that her future fortune may lie in accepting money for sexual favours. With that, she shows him the crown piece (surely far more than the astrologer himself would have earned for a single reading) and storms off in a temper. There is some ambiguity here.

The girl certainly appears more indignant at having been caught out than repentant for her deeds. The song's lyrics could even be taken to mean that the maid considered herself to have been well paid for her sexual liaison and had no need to mix with the likes of astrologers and conjurors, whom she considered to be beneath whoredom. There is also the unanswered question of whether the motive behind the astrologer's attempt to lure the maid upstairs is purely sexual, or actually part of a subterfuge to expose her hypocrisy. Either way the song neatly subverts the listener's expectations.

Zodiac (*Encyclopaedia Brittannia* 1771)

Joyce Froome puts it rather well in her notes to *Songs of Witchcraft and Magic* when she writes that the song 'exploits to the full the irony of the collision between the uncanny and the mundane'. However the lyrics are read, it is a fine piece of bawdy storytelling and somehow has a ring of truth, or at least authenticity about it. In *Popular Magic — Cunning Folk in English History* (2007), Owen Davies writes 'Whenever money mixes with the practice of magic, there will always be those who seek to exploit and defraud'. Perhaps likewise there will always be those who approach magic with cynical amusement, and who sometimes cannot handle the outcome!

music page 128

2. The Bells of Paradise

Down in yon forest there stands a hall:
The Bells of Paradise I heard them ring:
It's covered all over with purple and pall:
And I love my Lord Jesus above anything.

In that hall there stands a bed:
The Bells of Paradise I heard them ring:
It's covered all over with scarlet so red:
And I love my Lord Jesus above anything.

At the bed-side there lies a stone:
The Bells of Paradise I heard them ring:
Whih the sweet Virgin Mary knelt upon:
And I love my Lord Jesus above anything.

Under that bed there runs a flood:
The Bells of Paradise I heard them ring:
The one half runs water, the other runs blood:
And I love my Lord Jesus above anything.

At the bed's foot there grows a thorn:
The Bells of Paradise I heard them ring:
Which ever blows blossom since he was born:
And I love my Lord Jesus above anything.

Songs from the Magical Tradition

Over that bed the moon shines bright:
The Bells of Paradise I heard them ring:
Denoting our Saviour was born this night:
And I love my Lord Jesus above anything.

Also known as 'Down In Yon Forest', this traditional carol, which has become more popular in recent years, is one of the more ancient of its kind. This version, along with the tune (page 128) was collected by Ralph Vaughan Williams in 1908 in the village of Castleton, Derbyshire, though similar versions have been collected elsewhere. It is obviously related to the following poem in Middle English dating from around 1400.

> Lulley, lully; lulley, lully;
> The fawcon hath born my mak away.
>
> He bare hym vp, he bare hym down;
> He bare hym into an orchard brown.
>
> In that orchard ther was an hall,
> That was hangid with purpill and pall.
>
> And in that hall ther was a bede;
> Hit was hangid with gold so rede.
>
> And yn that bed ther lythe a knyght,
> His wowndes bledyng day and nyght.
>
> By that bedes side ther kneleth a may,
> And she wepeth both nyght and day.
>
> And by that beddes side ther stondith a ston,
> 'Corpus Christi' wretyn theron.

This anonymous poem contains elements of both the 'Bells of Paradise', and the 'Corpus Christi Carol', which seems to be a variant which according to legend was written down in the sixteenth century by a grocer's apprentice named Richard Hill, who found it in a damaged manuscript dated 1504. Richard Hill's *Commonplace Book* now resides in the library of Balliol College, Oxford.

At first sight the allusions in all the versions stem from Christian mysticism, the bed hung round with curtains being the altar, and the wounded knight the Eucharistic sacrifice, the body of Christ, whose

The Bells of Paradise

wounds from spear, nails and thorns do not heal. The hall itself could be the tomb of Christ. This interpretation sits happily with the fact that this may have originally been an Easter carol. The *may* (maid) in the poem presumably refers to Mary. In yet another version, collected by John Jacob Niles from Cherokee County, Carolina, the two repeated lines are 'Sing May, Queen May, sing Mary', and 'Sing all good men for the new-born baby' which also might indicate that a religious springtime song has here been reworked as a Christmas carol, perhaps around the time that carols were no longer generally sung at Easter. *Corpus Christi* (body of Christ) was a feast celebrated after Whitsun in honour of the Eucharist, so the carol, or at least the poem, may even date from the Middle Ages, though the tune used for the 'Bells of Paradise' does sound distinctly Tudor in style.

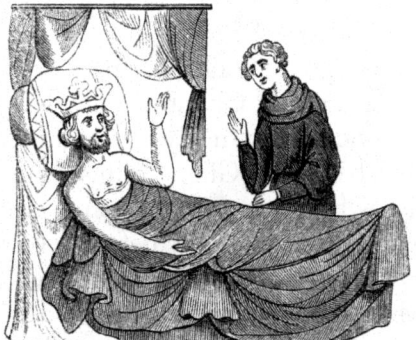

Illustration from *Hone's Every-Day Book* (1826)

The 'Bells of Paradise', the 'Corpus Christi Carol', and their variants have been much discussed, and many theories have been put forward as to their origin and meaning, some more sensible than others. One theory was that it was about Anne Boleyn, whose badge was a falcon, but as she was executed in 1536 this is hardly likely. There is yet another traditional folk song related to the carols, with slightly dark and mysterious lyrics, using the same tune with repeated lines of 'What are those bells that chime so clear?' and 'They are the Bells of Paradise'. Interestingly, this is lyrically quite different from the others, though it maintains the Easter/Christmas ambiguity, and although the mystical element is perhaps less strong, the line that includes the words 'matins rung from star to star' does lend it a rather other-worldy aspect.

In 1910, in the *Journal of the Folk-Song Society*, the folk song collector and expert Annie Gilchrist proposed a further interpretation based on the legends of the Holy Grail. She suggested that the scene described in the carol was similar to the thirteenth-century 'continuation' of Chretien de Troyes' unfinished *Perceval* attributed to Gerbert de Montreuil, in which the wounded King Mordrain lies bleeding in a forest chapel. The bleeding and dying knight may allude to the 'fisher king', the sacrificial king whose blood refreshes the land, while the rivers of blood and water, besides the obvious Biblical symbolism could possibly reference the red and white springs that run beneath Glastonbury Tor, the traditional mystical home of the Grail. The thorn 'at the bed's foot' too, seems to be a possible allusion to Glastonbury, where the famous thorn flowers around Christmas time. The occurrence of the maid and the stone next to the dying knight recalls the strange 'pretty maid' in the ballad of 'Giles Collins' who washed a stone in a stream, and has been compared to the 'washer at the ford' in Celtic mythology, who appeared before a battle washing the clothes of those who were about to die — perhaps a manifestation of the Goddess Morrighan — the 'Dark Queen'. Bob Stewart sees a clear progression of archetypal symbols with a strongly Celtic theme: wasteland; orchard; forest; bower; hall; blood; wounded man. To him, 'they are not merely historical remnants, but are images which arise in our minds, representing certain individual and generally human states of being.'

It is probably best not to analyse carols too much, they are some of our oldest folk songs and stem from an age when religion and magic were not mutually exclusive; when ordinary folk would worship God in church and invoke saints to enhance a spell at home. For this reason, much of their symbolism will always be ambiguous, but whatever religious allegiance we profess, we can always enjoy the poetry of their lyrics and the beauty of the music.

music page 129

3. The Boar's Head Carol

The boar's head in hand bear I,
Bedecked with bays and rosemary;
And I pray you, my masters, be merry,
Quot estis in convivio:

Caput apri defero,
Reddens laudes Domino.

The boar's head, as I understand,
Is the rarest dish in all this land,
Which thus bedecked with a gay garland,
Let us servire cantico:

Caput apri defero,
Reddens laudes Domino.

Our steward hath provided this
In honour of the King of Bliss;
Which, on this day to be served is,
In Reginensi atrio:

Caput apri defero,
Reddens laudes Domino.

Songs from the Magical Tradition

This carol, as printed above, is taken from the *Oxford Book of Carols*, compiled by Percy Dearmer, Ralph Vaughan Williams and Martin Shaw, first published in 1928. However, it was first printed thus in 1812 in Dibden's *Typographical Antiquities*, and several earlier versions are known. In the above form, it is still sung every Christmas at Queen's College, Oxford, with great pomp and ceremony, as part of the Yuletide celebrations. Dearmer gives the following translations from the Latin: *Quot estis in convivio* — 'So many as are in the feast'; *Caput apri defero reddens laudes Domino* — 'The boar's head I bring giving praises to God'; *servire cantico* — 'let us serve with a song'; *In Reginensi atrio* — 'In the Queen's Hall'.

William Henry Husk, secretary to the Sacred Harmonic Society, seems to have been a particular enthusiast for the carol, as he published no less than seven versions in his *Songs of the Nativity* in 1868. He included the earliest known printed version (1521), by Jan Van Wynken de Worde, the apprentice and successor to William Caxton. Husk notes that:

> The new version was in all probability made and introduced into use about the commencement of the last century, as it is palpably referred to by Hearne in a note on the older carol, which he printed amongst the "Notæ et Spicilegium," appended to his edition of William of Newbury's Chronicle of 1719 stating that "it will be perceived how much the same carol is altered as it is sung in some places even now from what it was at first."
>
> The ceremony now attending the bringing in the boar's head at Queen's College is as follows: The head (the finest and largest that can be procured) is decorated with garlands, bays, and rosemary, and is borne into the Hall on the shoulders of two of the chief servants of the college, and followed by members of the college, and by the college choir. The carol is sung by a member (usually a fellow) of the college, and the chorus by the choir as the procession advances to the high table, on reaching which, the boar's head is placed before the Provost, who sends slices of it to those who are with him at

the high table; and the head is then sent round to the other tables in the hall and partaken of by the occupants.

In his general introduction to boar's head carols, Husk writes of the boar's head feast in other contexts:

> The boar's head was brought to table with great ceremony; trumpeters preceded the bearer, sounding, and various other persons attended and formed a procession. Holinshed, in his Chronicle, acquaints us how King Henry II on the occasion of the coronation of his son Henry, as heir apparent, on the 14th June, 1170, himself brought up the boar's head, with trumpets before it. At Queen's College, Oxford, founded in 1340, the custom of bringing in a boar's head, on Christmas Day, with music and a carol (given hereinafter), has been preserved to our own times. At Henry's VI's coronation boar's heads were placed on the table in "castellys of golde and enamell." Margaret, daughter of Henry VII, and wife to James IV of Scotland, "at the furst course" of her wedding dinner, "was served of a wyld borres hed gylt, within a fayr platter.

Victorian facsimile of a miniature from the fourteenth-century manuscript *Livre du Roy Modus*

In Henry VIII's household accounts for 1529 there is an entry for 24 November, of a payment to a servant of the Lord Chamberlain of forty shillings 'in rewarde for bringing a wylde bore unto the king', and on New Year's Day, an identical sum was paid to one of the Lord Chamberlain's servants for a similar service. A servant of 'Maister Tresorer' received four shillings and eight pence on 18 December, 1531, 'for bringing a wylde bore's head to the king'.

Songs from the Magical Tradition

The custom continued throughout the reign of Elizabeth I, during which, on Christmas Day, in the Inner Temple, 'a fair and large boar's head' was served 'upon a silver platter with minstrelsy.' This continued into the reigns of her immediate successors, for Aubrey, in a manuscript, dated 1678, says: 'Before the last civil wars, in gentlemen's houses at Christmas, the first diet that was brought to table was a boar's head with a lemon in his mouth.'

Such goings-on at an ecclesiastical establishment such as Queen's College, which appear in spirit, at least, to be more than a little pagan, at first sight seem somewhat surprising, until one reads Pope Gregory's famous letter written to Abbot Melitus in 601, known as *The Deliberation of the Affair of the English,* in which he decreed that pagan temples should be 'purified' for re-use rather than destroyed, with Christian altars replacing the 'idols'. He extended this largess to a great deal more than the temples however; preserving at a stroke many pagan customs and ceremonies he wrote:

> because they have been accustomed to slaughter many oxen to devils, some solemnity must be exchanged for them on this account, so that on the day of the dedication, or the nativities of the holy martyrs, whose relics are there deposited, they may build themselves huts of the boughs of trees about those churches which have been turned to that use from temples, and celebrate the solemnity with religious feasting, and no more offer beasts to the devil, but kill cattle to the praise of God in their eating, and return thanks to the giver of all things for their sustenance.

Certainly the earlier versions of the carol which, fortunately, have survived are entirely secular in nature (as were many carols of the period), and seem to celebrate the feasting for its own sake, or for heroic reasons rather than for praising God. Edith Rickert identifies several early boar's head carols, including this one which was sung at St John's College, Oxford during the crowning of the 'Christmas Prince' — a sort of 'Lord of Misrule', or 'Master of the Revels', in 1607:

The Boar's Head Carol

The Boar is dead,
Lo, here is his head:
What man could have done more
Than his head off to strike,
Meleager like,
And bring it as I do before?

His living spoiled
Where good men toiled,
Where made kind Ceres sorry;
But now, dead and drawn,
Is very good braun,
And we have brought it for ye.

Then set down the swineyard,
The foe to the vineyard,
Let Bacchus crown his fall;
Let this boar's head and mustard
Stand for pig, goose, and custard,
And so you are welcome all.

The quasi-Classical allusions to Ceres, Bacchus and Meleager are typical of the Renaissance period, when a revival of paganism, albeit largely on an intellectual plane, became popular in academic circles. Also found in Rickert's *Ancient English Christmas Carols 1400-1700*, published in 1910, are some splendid versions in Old English, several of which, she claimed, dated from the fourteenth century, though unfortunately she does not give sources. One, however, crops up in Henry Vizetelly's *Christmas with the Poets* (1851), in which he claims the words were preserved in a fifteenth-century manuscript. It certainly has a ring of authenticity about it:

Hey! Hey! Hey! Hey!
The Boar's head is arméd gay.

The boar's head in hand I bring,
With garlands gay encircling,
I pray you all with me to sing,
With Hey! ...

Lords, knights, and squires,
Parsons, priests, and vicars,
The boar's head is the first mess, [dish]
With Hey! ...

The boar's head, as I now say,
Takes its leave and goes away,
Goeth after the twelfth day,
With Hey! ...

Then comes the second course with pride,
The cranes, the herons, the bitterns, by their side.
The partridges, the plovers, the woodcocks, and the snipe,
Larks in hot show, for the ladies to pick,
Good drink also, luscious and fine,
Blood of Allemaine, romnay, and wine, [German, Spanish wine]
With Hey! ...

Good brewed ale and wine, I dare well say,
The boar's head with mustard armed so gay,
Furmity for pottage, and venison fine,
And the umbles of the doe and all that ever comes in. [offal]
Capons well baked, with knuckles of the roe,
Raisons and currants, and other spices, too,
With Hey! ...

Edith Rickert was convinced of the pagan origins of such carols:

> The boar's-head carols are interesting as embodying a ceremony surviving from a pagan sacrificial feast. Numerous as are the versions, their general effect is strikingly similar. Two give an account of the killing of the beast, and one drags in Christian symbolism by comparing him to Christ.

Part of a boar-hunt scene — floor tiles from Bayeux Cathedral chapterhouse (Normandy, C14th). Drawn by Laurence Keen.

The Boar's Head Carol

Of course, the boar's head is hardly the most satisfying part of the animal in culinary terms, and its use must surely have been principally ceremonial in intent — the flesh from a pig's head would not have fed many at a feast. Presumably the brawn would have been served up alongside other cuts of the meat, but the main purpose of the head would be symbolic, in honouring the host of the occasion. Another carol, printed below, is sung from the point of view of the hunter serving up his prey to the assembled company, clearly boastful at having killed such a savage beast:

> Tidings I bring you for to tell,
> What me in wild forest befel
> When me must with a wild beast mell [meddle]
> With a boar so bryme. [fierce]
>
> A boar so bryme that me pursued,
> Me for to kill so sharply moved,
> That brymly beast so cruel and unrude, [savage]
> There tamed I him,
> And reft from him both life and limb.
>
> Truly, to show you that this is true,
> His head with my sword I hew,
> To make this day to you mirth new,
> Now eat thereof anon.
>
> Eat, and much good do it you;
> Take your bread and mustard thereto.
> Joy with me that I have thus done,
> I pray you be glad every one,
> And joy all in one.

The message conveyed here is clearly: 'here's the proof of my bravery, now eat and be merry, I wish you gladness and joy'. Such celebratory words are entirely appropriate given that hunting boar was a dangerous occupation and the head of the animal would have been seen as a trophy of no little status; in 885, according to the *Anglo-Saxon Chronicle*, King Carloman of the Franks, no less, was slain by a wild boar.

Songs from the Magical Tradition

Chambers' dictionary notes that the boar's head was the favoured dish at the great Yule festival of the Northmen, and certainly the sentiments expressed in the above carol would probably not have been out of place at the feasting in a Saxon or Viking hall, where the tusked animal's head would likely have symbolized sexual and physical prowess, and eating the animal's brawn would have magically transferred some of the beast's vigour to those present. In several versions of the carol, the 'rarest' feast in all the land becomes the 'bravest', which makes more sense in this context. In the Old English epic poem *Beowulf*, warriors wear boar-crested helmets into battle, and such ornaments have been occasionally found — notably a pair of shoulder clasps which probably adorned the clothing of a king, possibly the pagan King Redwald, which were among the treasure at Sutton Hoo.

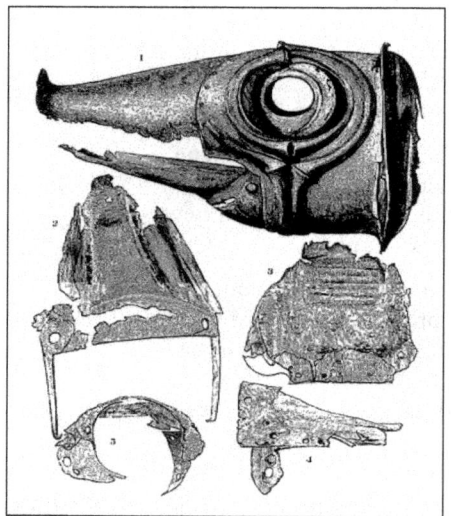

The Deskford Carnyx, discovered in 1816

The Celts, too, seem to have used images of the boar in a symbolic way, notably adorning the carnyx, or war-trumpet, boar-headed examples of which are illustrated on the Gundestrup Cauldron, and have been found occasionally; one very elaborate

The Boar's Head Carol

bronze example from Deskford in Banffshire had a wooden tongue, moveable by springs. The boar also appears on many Celtic coins, including those of the *Iceni*, and a few bronze figurines have also been found, such as the one near Findon in Sussex, which may indicate a Romano-British boar-hunting cult of some kind. Judging from the amounts of porcine bone found at Iron Age burial sites, eating pork was an important element of funerary rites. The northern British tribe known as the *Orci* (literally 'people of the boar') took their name from the animal.

Bedecking the boar's head with bay and rosemary, besides enhancing the flavour of the meat, may also be partially symbolic, as bay, otherwise known as laurel, has had connotations of regality and prowess in battle since Roman times, while rosemary is known as a herb of protection, love and friendship (see page 56); rosemary was, and sometimes is, used in folk magic to attract love, and for fertility.

It is possible that the tradition of serving a boar's head at a Christmas feast originated because the Germanic god Frey, or Freyr, who was responsible for the well-being of livestock, was symbolized by the boar. Therefore, a boar was often sacrificed in the hope of a successful spring herd in the new year, and its meat properly salted and stored, would provide sustenance throughout the winter months. Freyr became conflated with the Christian St Stephen in Britain and Scandinavia; his feast day is 26 December, which is of course, the most important date in the calendar for hunting. One Old English carol, 'Saint Stephen was a Clerk', has the saint himself bringing the boar's head to King Herod's feast. Even today, the Christmas ham is often saved to be eaten cold on Boxing Day, usually with mustard.

There is another tradition — that the boar's head ceremony in Oxford commemorates an act of bravery performed by a student of the college, who, walking in the neighbouring forest of Shotover while reading Aristotle, was suddenly attacked by a wild boar. The furious beast charged open-mouthed at the youth, who courageously, and with remarkable presence of mind, thrust the philosophical tome down the animal's throat, crying, "*Græcum est*," ["it is Greek" — possibly from the Latin proverb *Graecum est, non potest leg*i — 'it is Greek; it is unreadable'] and choked the savage creature to death with the words of the sage. This story appears to date no earlier than the eighteenth century, and the ballad in which the tale is found was probably written by the Revd Thomas Warton, who wrote a book of humorous and satirical verse about Oxford and its academic life in 1762.

***Bringing in the Boar's Head* by H. S. Marks (1871)**

The Boar's Head Carol, or rather carols, form a unique and fascinating insight into the medieval world; the fact that so many versions have survived is a testimony to the importance of the boar in the (Northern European) psyche as a fierce animal to be conquered by noble sporting endeavour, and also to the intriguing tenacity of some pre-Christian traditions.

music page 129

4. Childe Rowland

Childe Rowland and his brothers twain
Were playing at the ball,
And there was their sister Burd Ellen
In the midst, among them all.

Childe Rowland kicked it with his foot
And caught it with his knee;
At last as he plunged among them all
O'er the church he made it flee.

Burd Ellen round about the aisle
To seek the ball is gone,
But long they waited, and longer still,
And she came not back again.

They sought her east, they sought her west,
They sought her up and down,
And woe were the hearts of those brethren,
For she was not to be found.

So at last her eldest brother went to the Warlock Merlin and told him all the case, and asked him if he knew where Burd Ellen was.

"The fair Burd Ellen," said the Warlock Merlin, "must have been carried off by the fairies, because she went round the church 'wider shins'— the opposite way to the sun. She is now in the Dark Tower of the king of Elfland; it would take the boldest knight in Christendom to bring her back."

"If it is possible to bring her back," said her brother, "I'll do it, or perish in the attempt."

"Possible it is," said the Warlock Merlin, "but woe to the man or mother's son that attempts it, if he is not well taught beforehand what he is to do."

The eldest brother of Burd Ellen was not to be put off, by any fear of danger, from attempting to get her back, so he begged the Warlock Merlin to tell him what he should do, and what he should not do, in going to seek his sister. And after he had been taught, and had repeated his lesson, he set out for Elfland.

> But long they waited, and longer still,
> With doubt and muckle pain,
> But woe were the hearts of his brethren,
> For he came not back again.

Then the second brother got tired and sick of waiting, and he went to the Warlock Merlin and asked him the same as his brother. So he set out to find Burd Ellen.

> But long they waited, and longer still,
> With muckle doubt and pain,
> And woe were his mother's and brother's heart,
> For he came not back again.

And when they had waited and waited a good long time, Childe Rowland, the youngest of Burd Ellen's brothers, wished to go, and went to his mother, the good queen, to ask her to let him go. But she would not at first, for he was the last of her children she now had, and if he was lost, all would be lost. But he begged, and he begged, till at last the good queen let him go, and gave him his father's good brand that never struck in vain. And as she girt it round his waist, she said the spell that would give it victory.

So Childe Rowland said good-bye to the good queen, his mother, and went to the cave of the Warlock Merlin.

"Once more, and but once more," he said to the Warlock, "tell how man or mother's son may rescue Burd Ellen and her brothers twain."

"Well, my son," said the Warlock Merlin, "there are but two things, simple they may seem, but hard they are to do. One thing to do, and one thing not to do. And the thing to do is this: after you have entered

Childe Rowland

the land of Fairy, whoever speaks to you, till you meet the Burd Ellen, you must out with your father's brand and off with their head. And what you've not to do is this: bite no bit, and drink no drop, however hungry or thirsty you be; drink a drop, or bite a bit, while in Elfland you be and never will you see Middle Earth again."

The Victorian antiquary's archetypal image of the 'Warlock' Merlin: *Arch-Druid,* **by Charles Knight (1845)**

So Childe Rowland said the two things over and over again, till he knew them by heart, and he thanked the Warlock Merlin and went on his way. And he went along, and along, and along, and still further along, till he came to the horse-herd of the King of Elfland feeding his horses. These he knew by their fiery eyes, and knew that he was at last in the land of Fairy.

"Canst thou tell me," said Childe Rowland to the horse-herd, "where the King of Elfland's Dark Tower is?"

"I cannot tell thee," said the horse-herd, "but go on a little further and thou wilt come to the cow-herd, and he, maybe, can tell thee."

Then, without a word more, Childe Rowland drew the good brand that never struck in vain, and off went the horse-herd's head, and Childe Rowland went on further, till he came to the cow-herd, and asked him the same question.

"I can't tell thee," said he, "but go on a little farther, and thou wilt come to the hen-wife, and she is sure to know."

Then Childe Rowland out with his good brand, that never struck in vain, and off went the cow-herd's head. And he went on a little further, till he came to an old woman in a grey cloak, and he asked her if she knew where the Dark Tower of the King of Elfland was.

"Go on a, little further," said the hen-wife, "till you come to a round green hill, surrounded with terrace-rings, from the bottom to the top; go round it three times, widdershins, and each time say: "Open, door! open, door! And let me come in", and the third time the door will open, and you may go in.' And Childe Rowland was just going on, when he remembered what he had to do; so he out with the good brand, that never struck in vain, and off went the hen-wife's head.

Then he went on, and on, and on, till he came to the round green hill with the terrace-rings from top to bottom, and he went round it three times, widdershins, saying each time:

"Open, door! open, door! And let me come in."

And the third time the door did open, and he went in, and it closed with a click, and Childe Rowland was left in the dark.

It was not exactly dark, but a kind of twilight or gloaming. There were neither windows nor candles, and he could not make out where the twilight came from, if not through the walls and roof. These were rough arches made of a transparent rock, incrusted with sheepsilver and rock spar, and other bright stones. But though it was rock, the air was quite warm, as it always is in Elfland. So he went through this passage till at last he came to two wide and high folding-doors which stood ajar. And when he opened them, there he saw a most wonderful and glorious sight. A large and spacious hall, so large that it seemed to be as long, and as broad, as the green hill itself. The roof was supported by fine pillars, so large and lofty, that the pillars of a cathedral were as nothing to them. They were all of gold and silver, with fretted work, and between them and around them, wreaths of flowers, composed of what do you think? Why, of diamonds and emeralds, and all manner of precious stones. And the very key- stones of the arches had for ornaments clusters of diamonds and rubies, and pearls, and other precious stones. And all these arches met in the middle of the roof, and just there, hung by a gold chain, an immense lamp made out of one big pearl hollowed out and quite transparent. And in the middle of this was a big, huge carbuncle, which kept spinning round and round, and this was what gave light by its rays to the whole hall, which seemed as if the setting sun was shining on it.

The hall was furnished in a manner equally grand, and at one end

Childe Rowland

of it was a glorious couch of velvet, silk and gold, and there sate Burd Ellen, combing her golden hair with a silver comb. And when she saw Childe Rowland she stood up and said:

"God pity ye, poor luckless fool,
What have ye here to do?
Hear ye this, my youngest brother,
Why didn't ye bide at home?
Had you a hundred thousand lives
Ye couldn't spare any a one.

But sit ye down; but woe, O, woe,
That ever ye were born,
For come the King of Elfland in,
Your fortune is forlorn."

Then they sat down together, and Childe Rowland told her all that he had done, and she told him how their two brothers had reached the Dark Tower, but had been enchanted by the King of Elfland, and lay there entombed as if dead. And then after they had talked a little longer Childe Rowland began to feel hungry from his long travels, and told his sister Burd Ellen how hungry he was and asked for some food, forgetting all about the Warlock Merlin's warning.

Burd Ellen looked at Childe Rowland sadly, and shook her head, but she was under a spell, and could not warn him. So she rose up, and went out, and soon brought back a golden basin full of bread and milk. Childe Rowland was just going to raise it to his lips, when he looked at his sister and remembered why he had come all that way. So he dashed the bowl to the ground, and said: "Not a sup will I swallow, nor a bit will I bite, till Burd Ellen is set free."

Just at that moment they heard the noise of someone approaching, and a loud voice was heard saying:

"Fee, fi, fo, fum,
I smell the blood of a Christian man,
Be he dead, be he living, with my brand,
I'll dash his brains from his brain-pan."

And then the folding-doors of the hall were burst open, and the King of Elfland rushed in.

"Strike then, Bogle, if thou darest," shouted out Childe Rowland, and rushed to meet him with his good brand that never yet did fail. They fought, and they fought, and they fought, till Childe Rowland beat the King of Elfland down on to his knees, and caused him to yield and beg for mercy. "I grant thee mercy," said Childe Rowland, "release my sister from thy spells and raise my brothers to life, and let us all go free, and thou shalt be spared."

"I agree," said the Elfin King, and rising up he went to a chest from which he took a phial filled with a blood-red liquor. With this he anointed the ears, eyelids, nostrils, lips, and finger-tips, of the two brothers, and they sprang at once into life, and declared that their souls had been away, but had now returned. The Elfin king then said some words to Burd Ellen, and she was disenchanted, and they all four passed out of the hall, through the long passage, and turned their back on the Dark Tower, never to return again. And they reached home, and the good queen, their mother, and Burd Ellen never went round a church widdershins again.

The above is probably the most popular version of the story of Childe Rowland, as created by Joseph Jacobs in his *English Folk and Fairy Tales*, published in 1892. Its structure, part prose and part verse reflects the origins of the tale, as Jacobs used various fragments of an old Scottish ballad, 'Childe Roland and Burd Ellen', the first verses of which were published by Francis James Child. Sadly, the rest of the original ballad is lost, and Jacobs bulked out the surviving remnants with edited and rewritten extracts from Robert Jamieson's half-remembered version which had been published in *Illustrations of Northern Antiquities* (1814).

The first two verses, as published in Child's first collection in 1860, give a flavour of Jamieson's version:

> [KING Arthur's sons o' merry Carlisle]
> Were playing at the ba';
> And there was their sister Burd Ellen,
> I' the mids amang them a'.
>
> Child Rowland kick'd it wi' his foot,
> And keppit it wi' his knee;
> And ay, as he play'd out o'er them a',
> O'er the kirk he gar'd it flee.

Childe Rowland

Jamieson also translated a medieval Danish Ballad *Rosmer Hafmand*, which bears a striking similarity to the tale, though the Elf-king in this story is replaced by a mermaid. The only major difference in the storyline is that in the Danish version, the sister is unaware of her background until she is rescued by her brother.

At first sight, the story appears Arthurian, but in Child's version, printed above, 'King Arthur's sons of merry Carlisle' is bracketed, indicating that it is part of Jamieson's reconstruction, and the archetypal arch-druid/warlock/magician Merlin is not necessarily Arthur's legendary teacher and guide. Child himself notes that 'The occurrence of the name Merlin is by no means a sufficient ground for connecting this tale, [...] with the cycle of King Arthur [...] his name seems to have been given in Scotland to any sort of wizard or prophet'. Jamieson was an Arthurian enthusiast and in all probability the other Arthurian references (left out of Jacob's version) are also his. Burd Ellen may also have been introduced via Jamieson, from other, unconnected ballads.

Martin Carthy, in the sleeve notes to *Out of the Cut* (1982), opines: 'The King appears [in Jamieson's version] with Gwynivere and Excalibur as characters in the song but it seems to me that they are entirely superfluous and added later. [...] Alleged to have been sung or at least recited in ballad form by Jamieson's nurse to him when he was a little boy. From the narrative it would appear that the song would have been at least a couple of hundred lasting verses long, and one can only assume that Jamieson took a bloody age getting to sleep.' Carthy's own version, 'Jack Rowland' is notable for bringing in elements of magical transformation such as occur in the ballad 'The Two Magicians' (page 113); it still weighs in at a hefty thirty-nine verses!

More authentic sounding than the Arthurian references are the instructions given by Merlin to the young Rowland not to eat or drink anything while in the 'land of Fairy': Should a mortal enter the faerie realm and partake of any of the tempting fare offered, usually at a sumptuous feast, they will form a bond in the otherworld and become forever entrapped. This is a common thread in the folklore of Britain and Ireland, and also crops up in Classical mythology, notably in the story of Persephone, who after eating enchanted pomegranate seeds is trapped in the underworld and forced to remain there for half of each year while her mother Demeter mourns her annual departure. In a Cornish folktale a traveller is lost near Land's End and finds himself among a company of fairies. He recognizes the face of a girl among them — it is an old girlfriend whom he had thought dead. She explains that she was abducted, and a sham body buried in Buryan churchyard in her stead. She warns him not to eat or drink while among the fairies or a similar fate will befall him.

The beheading of the characters that Rowland encounters on his quest seems almost ritualistic, particularly as they are not in any way antagonistic, or even unhelpful to him. Several characters in fairy tales are transformed into animals by magic, and beg the hero to strike off their heads, at which point they return to human form. The occurrence of this motif here may indicate that all the characters in the 'land of Fairy' have actually been transformed in some way, presumably by the King of Elfland, and that the ultimate sacrifice is required to liberate them from this transformation, in a ritual, or even actual, death and rebirth. In a Norwegian tale seven foals revert to their former human form as princes after begging to be beheaded. In a medieval ballad *The Carle of Carlisle*, the 'Carle' declares after Sir Gawain has beheaded him: 'By nigromance thus was I shapen / Till a knight of the Round Table / Had with a sword smitten off my head.' In this case the Carle is transformed from an uncouth warrior to a chivalric Christian knight.

There are several theories as to the origins of faerie folklore. According to James MacKillop, these are principally that the stories enshrine a folk-memory of a region's original inhabitants; that they are the discarded gods and diminished heroes of an older religion; they are the personification of primitive nature spirits; or that they embody the spirits of the dead. The last of these would help to explain the taboo surrounding faerie food, while the first

Childe Rowland

would explain the location of the King of Elfland's hall as lying beneath a 'round green hill with the terrace-rings from top to bottom' — this sounds very much like an Iron Age hill-fort. One of the interesting features of many such earthworks is that temples were built within their confines in the fourth century, indicating a revival in pagan worship at a time when the nominally Christian Roman Empire was relinquishing its hold on the native British; memories of ancestral religious rites would almost certainly have been a factor in their siting. Other strong candidates for the hill with its 'dark tower' that the original ballad writer might have had in mind are the allegedly sculpted 'hollow hills' such as Glastonbury Tor or Burrow Mump, both of which lie firmly within the mythical landscape of Arthurian legend in the Somerset Levels.

Burrow Mump **by S. Cooper (1785)**

Ancient earthworks, particularly hill-forts and barrows are often cited as belonging to the realm of faerie. There are two barrows at Bincome in Dorset, where according to local folklore, faerie music may be heard at certain times of the day; within living memory at one of them, Culliford Tree Barrow, a woman was apparently warned twice not to purchase land adjacent to it by a mysterious disembodied voice.

The Church demonized the deities of the 'Old Religion' and many ancient sacred sites have therefore accrued folklore involving the devil. It is interesting to note that at many of these sites the devil may be 'called up' by running around a mound or hill 'widdershins' ('against the sun'), just as in this ballad Rowland circles the 'terrace rings' three times to gain entrance to the 'Land of Fairy'. A particularly interesting example of this, which seems to enshrine a faint folk-memory of ancient pagan ritual, occurs at Chanctonbury Ring in Sussex; in one version of the folklore, if you run around the hill seven times widdershins at midsummer, the devil will appear and offer food; Chanctonbury Ring is a late Bronze Age causewayed enclosure near Worthing, with a Romano-British temple at its centre.

The ballad of Childe Rowland was certainly current in Shakespeare's time, as he quotes from a version of it in *King Lear* (Act III, Scene 4):

"Childe Roland to the Dark Tower came,
His word was so still — Fie, foh, and fom,
I smell the blood of a British man."

Shakespeare's use of these lines is probably one of the principal reasons for the ballad's long-lived popularity as a resource for more modern literature: Stephen King wrote about a character named Roland in *The Dark Tower* (1982) in which Roland is the last gunslinger on a tireless mission to reach the Dark Tower, a nexus of all worlds; British fantasy author Alan Garner also drew heavily on the tale in his novel *Elidor* (1965), while American fantasy and science fiction author Andre Norton retold the fairy tale in her novel *Warlock of the Witch World* (1967). Robert Browning's 1855 doom-laden poem *Childe Rowland to the Dark Tower Came* takes its inspiration more directly from Shakespeare, and has virtually no connection with the early ballad. Probably one the best uses made of the tale in literature, is Lord Dunsany's *The King of Elfland's Daughter* (1924).

'Childe Rowland' is a fascinating ballad, and it is a shame that, unless a version turns up in some hitherto forgotten manuscript collection, we will probably never know its original form. I am greatly indebted to the late singer-songwriter Maria Cunningham for sending me her superb reconstruction, recorded in her collection of songs *Albion's Words* (see pages 129-131).

music page 132

5. Clerk Colvill

Clerk Colvill and his lusty dame
Were walking in the garden green,
The belt around her stately waist
Cost Clerk Colvill of pounds fifteen.

"O promise me now, Clerk Colvill,
Or it will cost ye muckle strife,
Ride never by the wells of Slane,
If ye wad live and brook your life."

"Now speak nae mair, my lusty dame,
Now speak nae mair of that to me;
Did I neer see a fair woman
But I wad sin with my body?'

He's taen leave o his gay lady,
Nought minding what his lady said,
And he's rode by the wells of Slane,
Where washing was a bonny maid.

"Wash on, wash on, my bonny maid,
That wash sae clean your sark of silk;"
"It's a' for you, ye gentle knight,
 My skin is whiter than the milk."

Songs from the Magical Tradition

He's taen her by the milk-white hand,
And likewise by the grass-green sleeve,
And laid her down upon the green,
Nor of his lady speer'd he leave.

Then loud, loud cry'd the Clerk Colvill,
"O my head it pains me sair;"
"Then take, then take," the maiden said,
"And frae my sark you'll cut a gare"

Then she's gied him a little bane-knife,
And frae her sark he cut a share;
She's ty'd it round his whey-white face,
But ay his head it aked mair.

Then louder cry'd the Clerk Colvill,
"O sairer, sairer akes my head"
"And sairer, sairer ever will,"
The maiden crys, "till you be dead"

Out then he drew his shining blade
Thinking to stick her where she stood,
But she was vanished to a fish
And swam far off, a fair mermaid.

"O mother, mother, braid my hair
My lusty lady, make my bed.
O brother, take my sword and spear
For I have seen the false mermaid."

There are very few genuinely old ballads about mermaids, though such beings do crop up in folk tales from all over the country, particularly in counties such as Cornwall, which have a strong seafaring tradition. This ballad is #42 in Child's *English and Scottish Ballads*, the only one of its kind in his collection. The version above is the one he gleaned from Herd's *Ancient and Modern Songs* (1769). In other versions the protagonist is named either Clerk Colven or

Clerk Colvill

Illustration by Arthur Rackham from *Some English Ballads* (1919)

Clerk Colin. In Britain, the ballad has only ever been collected in Scotland, though a related ballad, 'George [or Giles] Collins' has been found occasionally in England.

As Jean Renaud writes in the introduction to the 1904 edition of the *English and Scottish Ballads*:

> All the English versions [of Clerk Colvill] are deplorably imperfect [...] His history, were it fully told, would closely resemble that of the Knight of Staufenberg, as narrated in a German poem of about the year 1310. Clerk Colvill and the mermaid are represented by Sir Oluf and an elf in Scandinavian ballads to the number of about seventy. The oldest of these is derived from a Danish manuscript of 1550, two centuries and a half later than the Staufenberg poem, but two earlier than Clerk Colvill, the oldest ballad outside of the Scandinavian series (see Grundtvig, No. 47). The Breton 'Seigneur Nann' is closely akin to the Scandinavian versions, and the ballad has spread, apparently from Brittany, over all France.

More recently there have been attempts to link 'Clerk Colvill' with the ballad of 'Lady Alice'. A.L. Lloyd believed the two ballads were originally one, and that 'George Collins' is a more complete version of the combined storylines. In the latter a knight enjoys a tryst with a mysterious woman washing in a stream, which leads ultimately to his demise, along with his mortal lover and several other girls who afterwards die of sorrow. He explains:

> the vivid girl with the fatal kiss is a water-fairy, jilted and out for revenge. The theme has spread throughout Europe and has reached America, but there the meaning is lost, and the supernatural lover and the girl who mourns for Collins become one person, making the story banal. The mystery is there but some clues are missing, and the story is all the more dreamlike in consequence.

The stories of Clerk Colvill and George Collins appear to derive from an ancient legend, found in various forms across Europe. Child cites several examples, but actual mermaids do not appear in any of them, and the supernatural lover, though connected with water, is generally an elf of some kind. The commonest form of the legend is that a female water nymph, or undine, believes that in order to gain a soul she must marry a mortal man and bear a child. She falls in love with a human, but he deceives her by secretly becoming betrothed to another (human) woman. When the deception is discovered she takes revenge on her lover with a poisoned kiss, at which point the human bride-to-be also dies of a broken heart. It has been suggested that Child's Scottish versions were derived from a similar Faeroese ballad via Orkney and Shetland, islands where elves or undines are rare, but merfolk more common.

Robert Graves, in his inimitable manner, declared that originally the supernatural lover was a witch:

> In the original story, to judge from Scandinavian ballads, the girl is simply a witch. Mermaids do not, of course, either wear or wash bodices and the green sleeve of the Maid of

Clerk Colvill

Slane showed what she was clearly enough. Clerk Colvill's angry reply to his wife, who warned him to beware the wells of slane, suggests that he had been the young witch's lover before making a respectable marriage. When he tried to resume his former relations with her behind his wife's back, she took revenge by putting a death spell on him.

Graves suggests, with some justification, that later ballad singers mistook the witch for a mermaid simply because she transformed herself into a fish — shape-shifting being a fairly regular activity among witches. He also points out that a mermaid's natural element is salt water, whereas this one swam in the River Clyde.

Certainly, Clerk Colvill is not, as are the protagonists of many other ballads, a guiltless and guileless object of the love, or envy, of a supernatural being. It is clear that before his marriage to his 'gay lady' he had been in the habit of resorting to his mermaid lover, and it is equally clear that he means to visit her again. There is little attempt at deception by the two-timing womanizer, whose attitude to the fairer sex is indicated by his sneering boast to his wife that 'I never saw a fair woman, but with her body I could sin', and in this version it is the mermaid lover who exacts a terrible, but probably well-merited revenge. As Renauld wrote: 'His death is the natural penalty of his desertion of the water-nymph; for no point is better established than the fatal consequences of inconstancy in such connections.'

Mermaids do not always necessarily suffer as a result of their encounters with humans. In the legend of Zennor, in Cornwall, long ago, a richly dressed and beautiful lady occasionally attended the local church; no-one knew where she came from. After a service one Sunday, Matthew Trewella, a handsome young fellow with the best singing voice in the village, took it upon himself to discover who this mysterious stranger was, and he followed her as she left and made her way towards the cliffs.

That was the last anyone ever saw of Matthew or the strange lady. As the years passed his unexplained disappearance almost faded from memory. Then one Sunday morning, when a ship was anchored off Pendower Cove near Zennor, the captain heard a woman's voice hailing him from the water. Looking over the side of the ship he saw a beautiful mermaid, with her long blond hair flowing all around her. She asked if he would be so kind as to raise his anchor as it was resting upon the doorway of her house. She explained she was Morveren, one of the daughters of Llyr, king of the ocean, and she was anxious to get back to her beloved husband, Matthew, and her children.

The captain weighed anchor and headed for deeper water fearing the mermaid would bring the ship bad luck. He did, however, return later to tell the people of Zennor about Matthew's fate; the carving on the bench-end in the local church is said to be a warning to other young men not to go with mermaids.

The Mermaid in St Senara's church, Zennor.

music page 132

6. The Cutty Wren

O where are you going? said Milder to Mulder,
O we may not tell you said Festle to Fose
We're off to the woods said John the Red Nose,
We're off to the woods said John the Red Nose

What will you do there? said Milder to Mulder,
O we may not tell you said Festle to Fose
We'll hunt the Cutty Wren said John the Red Nose,
We'll hunt the Cutty Wren said John the Red Nose

How will you shoot her? said Milder to Mulder,
O we may not tell you said Festle to Fose
With bows and with arrows said John the Red Nose,
With bows and with arrows said John the Red Nose

That will not do then said Milder to Mulder,
O what will do then? said Festle to Fose
Big guns and big cannons said John the Red Nose,
Big guns and big cannons said John the Red Nose

How will you bring her home? said Milder to Mulder,
O we may not tell you said Festle to Fose
On four strong men's shoulders said John the Red Nose,
On four strong men's shoulders said John the Red Nose

Songs from the Magical Tradition

That will not do then said Milder to Mulder,
O what will do then? said Festle to Fose
Big carts and big waggons said John the Red Nose,
Big carts and big waggons said John the Red Nose

How will you cut her up? said Milder to Mulder,
O we may not tell you said Festle to Fose
With knives and with forks said John the Red Nose,
With knives and with forks said John the Red Nose

That will not do then said Milder to Mulder,
O what will do then? said Festle to Fose
Big hatchets and cleavers said John the Red Nose,
Big hatchets and cleavers said John the Red Nose

How will you cook her? said Milder to Mulder,
O we may not tell you said Festle to Fose
With pots and with pans said John the Red Nose,
With pots and with pans said John the Red Nose

That will not do then said Milder to Mulder,
O what will do then? said Festle to Fose
In a bloody great brass cauldron said John the Red Nose,
In a bloody great brass said John the Red Nose

Who'll get the spare ribs? said Milder to Mulder,
O we may not tell you said Festle to Fose
We'll give them all to the poor said John the Red Nose,
We'll give them all to the poor said John the Red Nose

The mysterious Cutty Wren song was collected by Cecil Sharp from a group of men in Adderbury, Oxfordshire in the early 1900s, sung to a tune known as 'Green Bushes'; a version had been published previously in M. Cooper's *Tom Thumb's Pretty Song Book* (*c*.1774). While the lyrics do sound a little like a children's question and answer song, akin to the 'Who Killed Cock Robin' nursery rhyme, the song was actually part of a serious traditional ritual custom which had survived against the odds in at least fifteen counties in England, and is also known to have taken place in similar form in Scandinavian countries, while Irish, Scots, Welsh and Manx versions of the song have since been collected. According to Iona and Peter Opie in *The Oxford Book of Nursery Rhymes* (1951) it is:

> A folk-chant of considerable curiosity, which was embodied in nursery rhyme books at an early date. It appears to be indigenous to all four kingdoms, and is likely to be exceptionally old. In Ireland the characters have been recorded as "O, Andhra Roe, Brothers-in-Three, and the Kriggerawee"; in Wales, "Dibyn, Dobyn, Risiart, Robin, John, a y tri"; in Scotland, "Fozie Mozie, Johnie Rednosie, Foslin 'ene, and brither and kin".

A version that does not actually include the wren is 'Cricketty Wee', a nonsense song collected in Ireland in 1937.

There is a Manx legend that during the Irish rebellion, when English soldiers and Manx Fencibles were in Ireland, the noise made by the wren on the end of a drum woke a sleeping sentry and thus saved them from being taken unawares (see also page 41); this has been given as a reason for hunting the wren on St Stephen's Day, but the widespread nature of the practice makes this seem highly unlikely.

The Oxfordshire wren-hunters had no idea why they performed such a rite, only that it 'had always been done', and were unaware of similar goings on in other parts of the country. The hunting of a wren, and occasionally its crucifixion, was at one time a common occurrence on St Stephen's day. This blatantly bizarre custom, and its song with lyrics which exaggerate the gravity of the act into the realms of the fantastical, at first sight seem to be completely nonsensical, and yet the form of the song's music, with its hypnotic rhythm and insistent beat, along with its (almost liturgical style) call-and-response lyrics hint that something altogether more serious is going on.

In societies where the written word was the privilege of the chosen few, chants and songs were, and in some cases still are, a useful mnemonic device for remembering the important lyrical content for significant ritual occasions. The call-and-response pattern of the song recalls the magical rituals of both 'primitive' and 'sophisticated peoples', from aboriginal hunting rites to the Catholic Mass. Bob Stewart, in *Where is St George?*, hints that the song may actually be a survival of a formal liturgical song from pre-Christian days. Certainly, the imagery of the song's perceived nonsensical lyrics might well have passed over the heads of the religious censors of the Middle Ages, even if no Christian interpretation of their content could satisfactorily be provided.

The protagonists in the song challenge and respond to each other's call, and their claims appear to be judged by the character 'John the Red Nose', who seems to be the final arbiter. The hunting of the wren, the smallest of birds seems to require enormous effort — bows and arrows are not sufficient, there must be big guns and cannon; four strong men cannot bear the weight of the prey — carts and wagons are needed, and so on. Thus the 'cutty' (little) wren is depicted as something small and yet at the same time very great. This may be an echo of the old folk tale in which the wren becomes the king of all the birds by stealth — simultaneously the smallest and yet the most important of creatures. This is a common enough motif in the western mystery tradition, with hints of 'as above, so below'.

The slaying of a king (see page 61), for which James Frazer claims the wren to be a symbolic substitute, is a well known if academically disputed part of ancient pagan religion, in which the king and the land are one, and the king must be sacrificed in order that the land can be renewed each year. Perhaps the exaggerated lyrics once served as a reminder that while the symbolic slaying of a tiny bird might seem a trivial thing, the actual import of the ritual had a massive significance — the survival of the local community no less. It is also worth noting that at any other time, apart from the wren hunt, it was considered extremely bad luck to kill a wren, and thus the timing of the ritual, usually around the winter solstice, was obviously crucial to its efficacy.

The common wren, engraving (1869)

The brass cauldron could be interpreted as a reference to the death and rebirth cycle of Celtic myths concerning the goddess Kerridwen the ancient mother, the source of divine wisdom and immortality. Thus the fertility aspect of the custom, the renewal of the land, is inextricably linked with not just the physical, but the spiritual survival and well-being of the community. The wren is also sacred to Taliesin in Celtic myth, and according to the antiquary Charles Vallency's magnum opus *Collecteana de rebus Hibernicis* (published between 1770 and 1806), the first Christian missionaries to Ireland took offence at the respect shown to the wren, and commanded that it be hunted and killed on Christmas Day.

The earliest written reference to wren-hunting is in Aubrey's *Miscellanea* (1690), which gives an unlikely explanation of the origins of the practice, given that it was once widespread throughout Europe:

> Near the same place, a party of the Protestants had been surprised sleeping by the Popish Irish, were it not for several wrens that just wakened them by dancing and pecking on the drums as the enemy were approaching. For this reason the wild Irish mortally hate these birds, to this day, calling them the Devil's servants, and killing them wherever they catch them; they teach their Children to thrust them full of thorns: you will see sometimes on holidays, a whole parish running like mad men from hedge to hedge a wren-hunting.

There have been other interpretations, but none has successfully explained the likely origins of the song. In his booklet *The Singing*

Englishman (1944), A.L. Lloyd suggested that 'The Cutty Wren' was a late-fourteenth-century song associated with the Peasants' Revolt of 1381. This was then regarded as a plausible hypothesis, but it was one for which no evidence was forthcoming, and as Lloyd was writing from a Marxist perspective at the time, it was (probably rightly) disregarded by most folklorists of the day. He was gracious enough to accept much of the criticism that was written about *The Singing Englishman* by eminent folk song collectors such as Maud Karpeles, and revized his opinions. In the meantime he seems to have become an advocate of Frazerian interpretation, for later, in *Folk Song in England* (1967), he wrote:

> We know that the wren-hunting song was attached to a pagan midwinter ritual of the kind that Church and authority fulminated vainly against — particularly in the rebellious period at the end of the Middle Ages when adherence to forms of the Old Religion was taken to be evidence of subversion, and its partisans were violently persecuted in consequence.

The Cutty Wren ceremony was revived in Suffolk in 1994, and is performed on the evening of St Stephen's day by the Old Glory molly dancers in the village of Middleton. A man dressed in Victorian agricultural clothes leads a procession of corduroy-clad men in hats, overcoats and hobnail boots; he has a blackened face and wields a broom, sweeping a path for the 'Lord' and 'Lady' (both male) who follow behind him, and a man carrying the carved effigy of a wren, hidden in a bush of ivy on a garlanded pole. The procession moves slowly to a drum beat, followed by the musicians and the villagers carrying lanterns in eager anticipation of the rite, which takes place outside the local pub. If the revived ceremony shows the influence of the nineteenth-century antiquaries and the modern Pagan movement, the song itself does seem to be a genuinely old one that hints at ancient pre-Christian magical practice. While its original purpose is obscure, the Cutty Wren is a marvellously atmospheric part of the magical tradition.

music page 133

7. Hal-An-Tow

Robin Hood and Little John,
They both are gone to the fair, O!
And we will go to the merry green-wood,
To see what they do there, O!
And for to chase, O!
To chase the buck and doe.

With hal-an-tow, rumble, O!
For we were up as soon as any day, O!
And for to fetch the summer home,
The summer and the may, O!
For summer is a-come, O!
And winter is a-gone, O!

Where are those Spaniards
That make so great a boast, O?
They shall eat the grey goose feather,
And we will eat the roast, O!
In every land, O!
The land where'er we go.

With hal-an-tow ...

As for Saint George, O!
Saint George he was a knight, O!
Of all the knights in Christendom,
Saint George is the right, O!
In every land, O!
The land were'er we go.

With hal-an-tow ...

God Bless Aunt Mary Moses,
With all her power and might, O!
And send us peace in Merry England,
Both by day and night, O!
And send us peace in Merry England,
Both now and evermore, O!

The Hal-An-Tow is one of Britain's oldest May Day rituals. It is performed at Helston in Cornwall on Furry Day (8 May), the feast of St Michael. 'Furry', in this context is often believed to be a corruption of 'Flora', from the floral garlands worn and carried during the proceedings — an interesting example of a seasonal custom being moved to accommodate a Christian saint's day, while retaining, albeit inadvertently, the name of a Roman goddess. Another, less exotic explanation is that 'furry' is derived from an old Cornish word signifying 'jubilee', or 'fair'. The better known Furry Dance, which also takes place on this day, certainly predates 1602, when it was described as 'flourishing'; most experts believe the Hal-An-Tow to be much older.

On the morning of St Michael's Day, all the participants congregate on the bridge over the River Cober, and the circular dance known as the Hal-An-Tow begins promptly at eight-thirty. The male dancers appear as 'men of the woods' and the women wear green ivy and may blossom. Others dress as the characters in the song, forming pretty much the standard cast of the English mumming tradition.

Hal-An-Tow

The Furry Day Song, an engraving published in 1922

In the early days of the Hal-An-Tow, the 'May Bride' was awoken by the blowing of whistles and banging of drums. A correspondent of the *Gentleman's Magazine*, for June 1790, wrote:

> In the morning, very early, some troublesome rogues go round the streets, with drums and other noisy instruments, disturbing their sober neighbours, and singing parts of a song, the whole of which nobody now recollects, and of which I know no more than there is mention in it of the 'grey-goose quill', and of going 'to the green wood' to bring home 'the Summer and the May O!' And, accordingly, hawthorn flowering branches are worn in hats. The commonalty make it a general holiday; and if they find any person at work, make him ride on a pole, carried on men's shoulders, to the river, over which he is to leap in a wide place, if he can; if he cannot, he must leap in, for leap he must, or pay money. About 9 o'clock they appear before the school, and demand holiday for the Latin boys, which is invariably granted; after which they collect money from house to house. About the middle of the day they collect together, to dance hand-in hand round the streets, to the sound of the fiddle, playing a particular tune, which they continue to do till it is dark. This they call a 'Faddy'.

Thus, it appears, the dance was actually known then as the 'Faddy'. Interestingly, the sycamore was known as the 'Faddy Tree'; local boys would make whistles from its branches for the festival. Deane and Shaw, in *The Folklore of Cornwall* (1975) assert that the 'Faddy' may be related to an ancient English dance, 'The Fading', and to the Irish *Rincce Fada*, or 'Long Dance', performed before King James I of England on his landing at Kinsale in 1601. The selection of sycamore may possibly be a symbolic representation of the horns or antlers worn in more archaic versions of such ceremonies. May blossom and ivy worn by the participants may represent the light and dark, or summer and winter aspects of the year. May is poised between winter and summer, and starting the proceedings on a bridge may also reflect the balance and the conflict between summer and winter to which the Church attached its metaphorical struggle of St Michael (or St George) and the dragon. Sabine Baring-Gould suggested the Hal-An-Tow was a surviving fragment of the old English May games, which encompassed the selection of a May King and Queen, a procession, morris dancing, a hobby horse, and a mumming play, which would include, as a celebration of the season, the characters of Robin Hood and Maid Marian:

> In the afternoon the gentility go to some farm-house in the neighbourhood, to drink tea, syllabub, &c., and return in a morris dance to the town, where they form a Faddy, and dance through the streets till it is dark, claiming a right of going through any person's house, in at one door, and out at the other. And here it formerly used to end, and the company of all kinds to disperse quietly to their several habitations: but latterly corruptions have in this, as in other matters, crept in by degrees. The ladies, all elegantly dressed in white muslins, are now conducted by their partners to the ballroom, where they continue their dance till suppertime; after which they all faddy it out of the house, breaking off by degrees to their respective houses. The mobility imitate their superiors, and also adjourn to the several public-houses, where they continue their dance till midnight.

Hal-An-Tow

By the Victorian period the Hal-An-Tow had incorporated the procession and revelry of the 'Mock Mayor of St Johns', St Johns being a mill village then just outside the town of Helston itself. The villagers were obliged to disburse the marauding revellers, or risk being thrown into the river. These riotous proceedings were, inevitably perhaps, eventually banned by the authorities in the late nineteenth century, and for a time the Hal-An-Tow ceased to be a part of the Flora Day celebrations.

The 'Faddy', or 'Furry Dance' itself, was, as it is now, a matter of considerable civic pride. As Robert Bell noted in his *Ballads and Songs of the Peasantry of England* (1857):

> During the festival the gentry, tradespeople, servants, &c., dance through the streets and thread through certain of the houses to a very old dance tune.

Perhaps by then the divide between the 'upper' and 'lower' orders, as noted in the extract from the *Gentleman's Magazine*, had become less distinct.

A sketch by A. Gascoigne Wildey, R.N., from *The Graphic* 18 May 1907, showing the Mayor and the Sheriffs of London participating in the dance

Songs from the Magical Tradition

The song lyrics printed above, are from Robert Bell's collection, with the final verse, which he left out, probably because he found it incomprehensible, from Baring-Gould. Eventually the Hal-An-Tow was revived in 1930 in a new version which included a verse celebrating both St George and St Michael and mentioning Helston, written by Robert Morton Nance, founder of the Old Cornwall Society and Grand Bard of the Cornish Gorsedd. The motto of the society was 'Gather ye the fragments that are left that nothing be lost'. Unfortunately this verse does little to enhance the song, and probably has little or nothing to do with its original meaning:

> But to a greater than St George,
> Our Helston has a right, O!
> St Michael with his wings outspread,
> The Archangel so bright, O!
> Who fought the fiend, O!
> Of all mankind the foe.

Nance thought the song likely to be no later than Elizabethan, as the words 'Hal-an-Tow, Rumble O' appear in a sixteenth-century sea shanty. Fortunately the tune survived to be published by William Sandys in 1846, and was later reused by Nance in his revived version of the song. There ensued considerable confusion between the Hal-An-Tow and the Furry Dance, and the two dances and their music were mistakenly conflated. Baring-Gould made this error in his *Songs and Ballads of the West* (1889), while the editors of the *Oxford Book of Carols* (1928) jumped through metronomic hoops to fit their 'Furry Day Carol' (a version of the Hal-An-Tow song) to the 'Helston Florey' tune published by antiquary Davies Gilbert in 1822! Further confusion ensued when a song by Katie Moss called 'The Floral Dance' was published in 1911, using a variant of the tune known as the 'North Cornwall Furry', which was later collected in Tintagel.

As to what 'Hal-An-Tow' actually means, no-one has come up with a completely convincing explanation. 'Haul and Tow', makes sense in terms of a sea shanty, especially if 'Rumble O!' is taken to mean 'Rum

Hal-An-Tow

Below', or it might be 'Heel and Toe' — a common dance figure in morris and step-dance traditions. In the mid seventeenth century one Cornish writer referred to the 'Haile-an-Taw'; *hayl* and *tyow* are Cornish for 'moor' and 'houses' respectively, so the chorus could be simply a celebration of countryside and town, brought together in May-time revelry. Mike O'Connor, in *Ilow Kernow 3* (2005), suggests *Halan To* in Cornish means 'the first day of the green harvest'.

Apart from the chorus, there is nothing specifically Cornish-sounding about the song itself, and it is quite possible that versions were sung at May revels throughout the country. It must be remembered, however, that Cornish culture took a severe blow after the 'prayer-book rebellion' in Henry VIII's time, which led ultimately to the suppression of the language, so whatever songs were sung at Helston in pre-Tudor times will have been lost, or at the very least mangled in translation, as may be the case here. Padstow, of course, has similar May festivities, though the 'Padstow May Song' is, for the most part, quite different.

Robin Hood and Little John appear in many songs associated with May-time festivities, and also in folk plays all over England. The verse referring to the Spaniards commemorates the many raids made by marauding Spanish ships on the Cornish coast, and celebrates the skill of the longbowmen who opposed them (goose feathers were used to fletch their arrows). St George may also have a local connotation — according to legend the town, which was once the resort of fiery dragons, is named after a large stone which the Devil threw at St Michael. As usual, he missed, and the stone landed in the courtyard of an inn. Today its fragments may be seen built into the back wall of the Angel public house; St George, the famous dragon-slayer is often conflated with St Michael, the scourge of paganism and the saint of high places.

The last, and perhaps the oddest verse introduces Aunt Mary Moses, who appears nowhere else in folklore. She may possibly be the Virgin Mary, for the Cornish word for a 'maid' or 'virgin' is *mowse*, so that 'Mary Mowse' could be be 'Mary the Virgin'. This may have been a sop to the local clergy for whom blessing 'Maid Marian', as the May Queen, would have seemed like condoning revenant paganism. It has also been suggested that the name was substituted for that of the monarch of the realm during the Commonwealth period, and was never altered back.

The song reproduced in the music section at the back of this book (see page 133) is not the one sung at Helston. It is an amalgam of several versions, as sung by the Watersons on their seminal *Frost and Fire* album. Since the 1960s this has become a fairly 'standard' rendition sung at May celebrations, and in folk clubs, throughout Britain. The second verse is taken almost verbatim from a song used by Shakespeare in his play *As You Like It* (1597). This verse harks back to the time when animal skins and horns were regularly worn in seasonal folk-ceremonies, a known practice in the Middle Ages which was soundly condemned by the Church on many occasions. The only genuine survivor into modern times of such folk customs appears to be the Abbots Bromley Horn Dance, in Staffordshire (see music page 142).

In the context of a song that may be a remnant of an ancient rite of Summer, and whose surviving verses probably date from Elizabethan times, this 'borrowing' from Shakespeare works remarkably well. This and the introductory verse were added by Mike Waterson himself in the 1960s. While such modern adaptations may cause some consternation among academic folklorists, perhaps they should be comforted by the enthusiasm their study has engendered among contemporary folk-singers and dancers, who have accepted their speculative conclusions and sought to reconstruct a ceremonial song in such an effective and 'authentic' manner.

music page 134

8. Jennifer Gentle

There were three sisters, fair and bright,
Jennifer gentle, fair Rosie Marie,
Wanted to wed with a valiant knight.
As the dew flies over the mulberry tree.

The eldest sister took him in,
Jennifer gentle, fair Rosie Marie,
Also bolted the silver pin.
As the dew flies over the mulberry tree.

The second sister made his bed,
Jennifer gentle, fair Rosie Marie,
Placed the pillow right under his head.
As the dew flies over the mulberry tree.

But the youngest sister, fair and bright,
Jennifer gentle, fair Rosie Marie,
Wanted to wed with the valiant knight.
As the dew flies over the mulberry tree.

Well, if you will answer my questions three,
Jennifer gentle, fair Rosie Marie,
Then, fair maid, I would marry thee.
As the dew flies over the mulberry tree.

Songs from the Magical Tradition

Oh, what is whiter than the milk?
Jennifer gentle, fair Rosie Marie,
What is softer than the silk?
As the dew flies over the mulberry tree.

Oh, snow is whiter than the silk;
Jennifer gentle, fair Rosie Marie,
Down is softer than the silk.
As the dew flies over the mulberry tree.

And what is sharper than the thorn?
Jennifer gentle, fair Rosie Marie,
What is louder than the horn?
As the dew flies over the mulberry tree.

Oh, hunger is sharper than the thorn,
Jennifer gentle, fair Rosie Marie,
Thunder's louder than the horn.
As the dew flies over the mulberry tree.

And what is broader than the way?
Jennifer gentle, fair Rosie Marie,
What is deeper than the sea.
As the dew flies over the mulberry tree.

Oh, love is broader than the way;
Jennifer gentle, fair Rosie Marie,
Hell is deeper than the sea.
As the dew flies over the mulberry tree.

Well, now you've answered my questions three;
Jennifer gentle, fair Rosie Marie,
Now, fair maid, I would marry thee.
As the dew flies over the mulberry tree.

Jennifer Gentle

This is a song common in British folk tradition in various versions, including 'The Three Sisters' or 'Riddles Wisely Expounded'. This version was published in 1822 by the Cornish antiquary Davies Gilbert in his collection *Some Ancient Christmas Carols with the Tunes to Which they were Formerly Sung in the West of England, Together with Two Ancient Ballads, a Dialogue, &c*. It bears the distinction of being the first ballad to be featured in Francis James Child's extensive collection *The English and Scottish Ballads* (1882-1896). Child included five different versions, though he printed Gilbert's, as he admitted, 'from the editor's recollection', incompletely.

The narrative of the song is very simple — three sisters conspire so that the youngest can marry a knight, who in another version of the song is both 'of noble worth', and 'of courage stout and brave'. They invite him in and seal the door, seemingly bringing an element of coercion to the proceedings. The knight agrees to wed the youngest daughter, but only if she can answer three questions, in the form of riddles, which she duly does.

Riddles are a very ancient device in mythology — the tales of Oedipus, Samson, and Apollonius of Tyre are all obvious examples. As a device to illustrate a battle of wits between two opposing characters they are invaluable in storytelling and folk ballads. John Porter writes that 'Riddle is metaphor, transformation and analogy, poetic perception, verbal play, language under creative imagination, 'making it new'. Whether as child's game, mythic repository, or lyric poem, [...] the riddle re-fashions vision by showing things stranger than they seem. It reveals by disguise, confuses to illumine, unifies the disparate through paradox.' Bob Stewart considers riddling to be 'magical in origin, and in content'.

The answers to the riddles bring to mind the verses of the Welsh Triads, which have been interpreted as mnemonic devices for passing on ancient and/or secret bardic knowledge, though it would be difficult to put any such interpretation into this song.

Songs from the Magical Tradition

There are a number of Irish and Scots ballads, such as 'The Devil's Nine Questions', which leave out the narrative story of the sisters and the knight altogether and concentrate on the riddles alone. The earliest such version in English dates from the middle of the fifteenth century and survives in a manuscript in the Bodleian Library with the Latin title *Inter Diabolus et Virgo* — 'Between a Maid and a Devil'. Here the riddles form a contest 'betwyxt a mayd and the fovle fende'. The maid is able to escape the clutches of the 'foul fiend' by correctly solving the riddles. Likewise in another of Child's versions the knight turns out to be the Devil in disguise, and the maid banishes him when she reveals his name in the answer to the final riddle. 'as sune as she the fiend did name, he flew awa in a blazing flame.'

Child identifies three classes of folk tale involving such riddles:

> The largest class of these tales is that in which one party has to guess another's riddles, or two rivals compete in giving or guessing, under penalty in either instance of forfeiting life or some other heavy wager; an example of which is the English ballad, in modern form of 'King John and the Abbot of Canterbury.' In a second class, a suitor can win a lady's hand only by guessing riddles, as in our 'Captain Wedderburn's Courtship' and 'Proud Lady Margaret.' There is sometimes a penalty of loss of life for the unsuccessful, but not in these ballads. Thirdly, there is the tale (perhaps an offshoot of an early form of the first) of The Clever Lass, who wins a husband, and sometimes a crown, by guessing riddles, solving difficult but practicable problems, or matching and evading impossibilities.

The repeated lines bring to mind 'Parsley, Sage, Rosemary and Thyme' of the 'Elfin Knight', another mysterious and ancient traditional song to which the song is certainly related. The principle theme is a variant of Child's third scenario — by posing 'impossible' tasks, the woman protagonist keeps her unwanted lover (the Elfin Knight — possibly a devil in disguise) at arm's length.

If, as Child suggests is likely, the chorus line is derived from 'juniper, gentian and rosemary', rather than being the names of

Jennifer Gentle

Medieval Herb Garden, from a German woodcut

the three sisters, as Gilbert infers, then the song may have strong connotations of herbal magic and folklore, as all three herbs, besides having a long history of medicinal usage, are also used in herbal magic, principally in love and protection spells. Pins were also used in amulets for such charms, and silver frequently crops up in similar contexts in traditional songs and ballads. Clearly a silver pin would be of little use in physically sealing a door, and therefore its use in this context must be magical, or symbolic. Silver often represents the moon in folklore, and so there may be an element of lunar magic involved here in producing a binding spell, the planting and use of herbs being inextricably linked to the moon and its cycles. In the three other versions in Child's collection broom is mentioned in the chorus — a magical plant associated with the fairies; the word 'gentle' is sometimes used in Ireland for 'hawthorn'. Regarding the slightly bewildering line 'the dew flies over the mulberry tree', the word 'dew', has been interpreted as being a corruption of 'dow', meaning 'dove', which certainly makes the line more comprehensible.

Lucy Broadwood, writing in the *Journal of the Folklore Society* in 1908, discusses 'magic flower refrains', as she terms them, in both this song and 'The Elfin Knight' (Child #2):

> Both abroad and in the British Isles one meets still with so many instances of plants being used as charms against demons, that I venture to suggest that these "plant-burdens", otherwise so nonsensical, are the survival of an incantation used against the demon suitor [...] from earliest times, the herbs or symbols efficacious against the evil eye and spirits, are also invariably used on the graves of the dead, or during the laying of the dead to rest.

English Woman Gathering Herbs —**Victorian engraving**

Rosemary was often burned inside a house as protection from, or banishment of, witchcraft. On a lighter note, it was also used in charms for love, and friendship — significantly, in the Middle Ages, sprigs were exchanged at marriage ceremonies along with rings. Sir Thomas More (1478-1535) wrote 'As for rosemary, I let it run all over my garden walls, not only because my bees love it but because it is the herb sacred to remembrance and to friendship, whence a sprig of it hath a dumb language.' Shakespeare's Ophelia gives Hamlet rosemary with the words 'There's rosemary, that's for remembrance; I pray you, love, remember'.

music page 134

9. John Barleycorn

There came three men out of the West,
Their victory to try;
And they have taken a solemn oath,
Poor Barleycorn should die.

They took a plough and ploughed him in,
And harrowed clods on his head;
And then they took a solemn oath,
Poor Barleycorn was dead.

There he lay sleeping in the ground,
Till rain from the sky did fall:
Then Barleycorn sprung up his head,
And so amazed them all.

There he remained till Midsummer,
And looked both pale and wan;
Then Barleycorn he got a beard,
And so became a man.

Then they sent men with scythes so sharp,
To cut him off at knee;
And then poor little Barleycorn,
They served him barbarously.

Songs from the Magical Tradition

Then they sent men with pitchforks strong
To pierce him through the heart;
And like a dreadful tragedy,
They bound him to a cart.

And then they brought him to a barn,
A prisoner to endure;
And so they fetched him out again,
And laid him on the floor.

Then they set men with holly clubs,
To beat the flesh from his bones;
But the miller he served him worse than that,
For he ground him betwixt two stones.

O! Barleycorn is the choicest grain
That ever was sown on land;
It will do more than any grain,
By the turning of your hand.

It will make a boy into a man,
And a man into an ass;
It will change your gold into silver,
And your silver into brass.

It will make the huntsman hunt the fox,
That never wound his horn;
It will bring the tinker to the stocks,
That people may him scorn.

It will put sack into a glass,
And claret in the can;
And it will cause a man to drink
Till he neither can go nor stand.

Sabine Baring-Gould and Cecil Sharp are largely responsible for the widespread dissemination of 'John Barleycorn' in the twentieth century, having included the song in their publication

John Barleycorn

English Folk Songs for Schools. Cecil Sharp collected several versions from singers in Devon and Somerset.

The version (titled 'Sir John Barleycorn') above is from Robert Bell's *Ancient Poems, Ballads and Songs of the Peasantry of England* (1857). Bell considers this to be an ancient West Country version of the ballad, it being 'the only version that has ever been sung at English merry-makings and country feasts [and is] very appropriately sung to the tune of Stingo' (see page 134). This tune, also known as 'The Oyle of Barley', is found in John Playford's *Dancing Master* published in 1651. Stingo was a slang word for strong ale in the seventeenth century, at which time there was a famous public house named the Yorkshire Stingo in Marylebone, London.

An article by Peter Wood, in *The Folk Music Journal* (2004) gives a picture of how a whole group of related songs developed through a series of re-makings from a sixteenth-century ballad. The earliest known version barely mentions the death-and-resurrection theme, the bulk of which seems to be a rather later addition possibly in the eighteenth century, when the revival of Classical studies led to a growth of interest in such things. Robert Burns reworked a version of the song in the 1780s, but according to Baring-Gould he 'in no way improved it', and fortunately more traditional versions have prevailed among folksingers.

The earliest known version, found in the *Bannatyne Manuscript*, dates to before 1568. It is in a Scots-Gaelic/Anglo-Norman-French dialect, and is called 'Allan O' Maut'. The first known English version, as noted by Pepys, has the not very snappy title 'A Pleasant New Ballad to Sing Evening and Morn, of the Bloody Murder of John Barleycorn'. Other versions had the titles 'Three Knights North', or, 'Three Men West'. Most versions have 'crabtree sticks' instead of 'holly clubs'. Later versions, such as that enshrined by the *Penguin Book of Folksongs* were much shorter, and it is generally in this form that the song is sung today (though there are still significant variations). It is this version (recorded by the rock band Traffic in 1970) that is featured on page 135.

Songs from the Magical Tradition

The legendary Shropshire folk-singer Fred Jordan sang a variant to the nineteenth-century German hymn tune 'We Plough the Fields and Scatter'. Interestingly in his version the three men in the first verse 'came out of Kent'; it also had a chorus:

> Come put your wine into glasses,
> Put your cider into old tin cans,
> Put Barleycorn in the nut-brown bowl
> And he'll prove the strongest man

Steeleye Span's version, collected in Bedfordshire, describes the actual brewing process, as does the earliest ballad version. The eighteenth-century broadsides leave this part out.

Before the harvest became fully mechanized, rural communities invested the cutting of the corn, particularly the last sheaf, with great ceremony. In Devon and Cornwall such harvest rites were known as crying the neck. Broadly, for there were many local variations, the reapers would form a circle around the most senior of them (sometimes referred to as the Harvest Lord), carrying aloft the last ears of corn to be cut. He would shout 'I havet, I havet, I havet', to which the response was 'What havee, what havee, what havee?' The response would be 'a neck, a neck, a neck, we have one' repeatedly, followed by much cheering from the assembled company. Finally, a cry of 'we yen, we yen, we yen' was raised, after which much merrymaking would ensue.

Wood engraving by Michael Manning

John Barleycorn

William Hone's *Every-Day Book* (1826), records the thoughts of a gentleman farmer regarding the ceremony. The final line of this extract seems perhaps to betray a slight feeling of unease that the narrator feels about participating in so pagan a custom:

> On a fine still autumn evening [it had] a wonderful effect at a distance. I have once or twice heard upwards of twenty men cry it, and sometimes joined by an equal number of female voices. About three years back, on some high grounds where our young people were harvesting, I heard six or seven 'necks' cried in one night, although I know that some of them were four miles off. They are heard throughout the quiet evening air, at a considerable distance sometimes. But I think the practice is beginning to decline of late, and many farmers and their men do not care about keeping up this old custom. I shall always patronise it myself, because I take it in the light of a thanksgiving.

The final sheaf would be decorated with ribbons and borne home in great triumph. Often an effigy in the form of a corn dolly was created by weaving the stalks together, which would be present at the harvest home celebrations, which usually consisted of feasting and dancing (there are several traditional dance tunes with the title 'Harvest Home' — see pages 143 and 146); traditionally, the corn dolly would often be kept either until the next year's harvest, or ploughed back into the ground with the next planting. It was from this, and similar customs throughout this country and elsewhere, that Sir James Frazer formed the idea of a symbolic 'corn king', whose annual sacrifice was necessary to ensure the vitality of the following year's crops, as being an essential element in primitive religion.

At Hitchen, Hertfordshire, in a related custom, when the last cartload of corn was harvested, it would be driven through the streets of the town, and local people would run alongside sprinkling it with water. This was apparently to ensure a plentiful supply of rain the following spring to aid the germination of the next crop.

Whether or not Frazer was correct in his assumption, the

elements of 'sympathetic magic' enshrined in harvest customs do require a form of embodiment of the spirit of the corn, and John Barleycorn provides this admirably. To quote from the sleeve notes of the Watersons' *Frost and Fire* album (1965):

> Sometimes called The Passion of the Corn. It's such an unusually coherent figuration of the old Frazerian myth of the Corn-King cut down and rising again, that the sceptical incline to think it may be an invention or refurbishing carried out by some educated antiquary. If so, he did his work long ago and successfully, for the ballad was already in print in the early years of the seventeenth century, and it has been widespread among folk singers in many parts of the English and Scottish countryside.

Kathleen Herbert, in her *Looking for the Lost Gods of England* (1994), makes a connection between the sacrificial figure in the song and the mythical Anglo-Saxon Beowa, who was associated with agriculture, *beowa* being Old Norse for 'barley', while other writers have seen John Barleycorn as the Celtic sun-god Lugh, whose festival, *Lughnasadh* was equivalent to the Old English Lammas ('loaf-mass') celebrations at the start of August. It is probable that harvest ceremonies enshrining the myth of some kind of corn-spirit existed in some form in most cultures, the myth of Osiris in ancient Egypt being one of the earliest recorded. John Barleycorn is our indigenous corn king, and his story is one of the most ancient and long-lived of the myths that survive in the magical tradition.

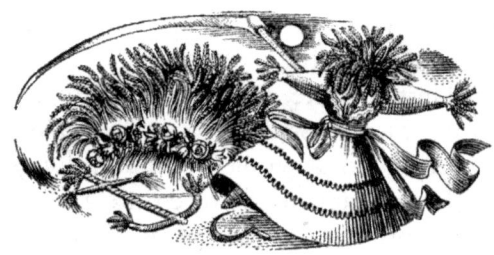

music page 136

10. King Orfeo

There was a King lived in the West,
Green the woods so early,
Of all the harpers he was the best,
Where the hart goes yearly.

The King he has a-hunting gone,
Green the woods so early,
And left his lady all alone,
Where the hart goes yearly.

The King of Faerie with his dart,
Green the woods so early,
Has pierced the lady to the heart,
Where the hart goes yearly.

So after them the King has gone,
Green the woods so early,
Until he came to a large grey stone,
Where the hart goes yearly.

And he took out his harp to play.
First he played the notes of pain,
And all their hearts were weary,
Then he played the Faerie reel,
And all their hearts were cheery.

Songs from the Magical Tradition

The King of Faerie, with his rout,
Green the woods so early,
Has gone to hunt him all about,
Where the hart goes yearly.

"Come ye into the Faerie hall,
Green the woods so early,
And play your harp amongst us all,"
Where the hart goes yearly.

And he took out his harp to play.
First he played the notes of pain,
And all their hearts were weary,
Then he played the Faerie reel,
And all their hearts were cheery.

"Oh what shall I give you for your play?"
Green the woods so early,
"Oh let me take my lady away."
Where the hart goes yearly.

The Faerie King said "Be it so,
Green the woods so early,
Take her by the hand and go."
Where the hart goes yearly.

And he took out his harp to play.
First he played the notes of pain,
And all their hearts were weary,
Then he played the Faerie reel,
And all their hearts were cheery.

This is probably the best-known version of *King Orfeo*, as recorded by Steeleye Span in 1976 for their classic album *Rocket Cottage*. The song, on which Maddy Prior sings a duet with herself, is a version of the ballad of the same name (#19) in Child's collection *The English and Scottish Popular Ballads*. Child's version a curious mixture of Scots and Shetlandic dialect, and

King Orfeo

was first published in 1880, in *The Leisure Hour*, having been collected from an old man in Unst, Shetland, by Biot Edmonston; the repeated lines in this version are the English translation from the dialect, as printed in the *Oxford Book of Ballads*. Despite the original ballad-poem being set in Wessex, the song has only ever been collected in the Shetlands, and infrequently at that, so it is fortunate that two tunes associated with the lyrics have survived, both of which appear to be medieval.

The origins of the ballad of King Orfeo appear to lie in an anonymous ballad-poem in Middle English called 'Sir Orfeo', a medieval retelling of the story of Orpheus and Eurydice, in which Greek mythology is merged with Celtic folklore; the earliest version is in a rare English secular codex known as the the Auchinleck Manuscript, which has been dated to around the late thirteenth or early fourteenth century and survives in the National Library of Scotland. It was probably based on a French source, the *Lai d'Orphrey* which was possibly written by Marie de France and based on a Breton minstrel lay. The original tale was derived from classical texts such as Boethius, Virgil or Ovid, who all interpreted the original legend, which enshrines fragments of the Orphic and Eleusinian mystery religions of ancient Greece and Rome. Noel Williams suggests that the Middle English writer Walter Map may have introduced elements from the Anglo-Saxon tradition found in King Alfred's translation of Boethius, and that 'the Auchinleck romance may therefore contain elements from Classical Latin, Medieval Latin, Old French, Old English, Breton and Middle English traditions'. To this list one may add, from the sung version of the ballad, elements of a Shetlandic tradition heavily influenced by Scandinavia, in language at least.

In the manuscript, Queen Heurodis, instead of dying and descending to Hades like Eurydice, is carried off by the King of Elfland, from whose unwelcome attentions she is successfully rescued by her husband's virtuososic musical skills. The poem neatly replaces the Greek Hades with the Celtic 'otherworld' and introduces several other motifs from British mythology. A version translated by J.R.R. Tolkien was published posthumously along with 'Sir Gawain and the Green Knight' in 1944. Interestingly, the ballad version has Sir Orfeo holding court at Thrace, which is described as the old name for Winchester, the Anglo-Saxon capital of the Kingdom of Wessex. Orfeo left his estate in the hands of a trusty steward and set off to find his lady. He spent ten long years in the wilderness, with his harp being his only solace. Eventually he found her with a faerie hunting party, and having posed as a poor minstrel to gain entry to the castle, he is able to woo the King of Elfland into releasing his queen. When he returned incognito from his adventure he announced to his steward 'I am a harper from heathendom' (*Ich am an harpour of hethenisse*). The steward welcomed him, proving that his enthusiasm for music was true and undimmed by his master's long absence, whereupon Orfeo made himself known, and the assembled company fell at his feet.

A Knight Visiting a Faerie House, **by Olaus Magnus (1555)**

The motif of the faerie 'raiding', or 'hunting', party abducting mortal folk is a recurring one in British folklore and crops up in other traditional ballads such as 'Tam Lin', and 'Thomas the Rhymer'. The reference to the 'great grey stone' as being a portal to Elfland is an important one; standing stones are often associated with the realms of faerie and magic, and were venerated as sacred by the rural population well into the Middle Ages, as several, frequently quoted, edicts from the Church bemoaning such pagan recidivism attest. In the poem the lady is taken 'despite her will to live with him beneath the hill', suggesting that the King of Elfland's hall perhaps lay beneath a barrow or burial mound. Such sites have often been associated with so-called 'fairy music', which in folklore charms the listener, often with disastrous consequences, into entering the otherworld. In Dorset fairy music can be heard at mid-day at two Bronze Age barrows at Bincombe (see page 29), while folklore surrounding the great Irish harp player and composer Turlough Carolan suggests that he received his talent from the faerie folk while lying on a 'rath', or fairy mound. A tune which is regarded as his first composition, *Sheebeg and Sheemore* (trans. 'the big fairy hill and the little fairy hill'), was written about two such mounds that are said to commemorate a battle in antiquity between two rival faerie clans (see music page 145).

An unusual feature of this story is that, to a degree, the roles are reversed: King Orfeo, a mere mortal, is on this occasion able to charm the supernatural faerie folk into letting him enter Elfland and rescue his lady by using the magical agent of music, specifically by playing the 'Faerie Reel', though in Child's version the tune is not named, simply being described as a 'god gabber' (rollicking) reel. There are several traditional tunes known as the 'Fairy Reel', or the 'Fairy Dance', probably the best known being the one published in the late eighteenth century in Nathaniel Gow's collection of Scottish fiddle tunes, from which most Irish and American variants seem to have sprung (see music page 143). It is also known simply as 'The Fairy', or sometimes as 'Old Molly Hare', and is often used as a morris dance tune in England.

The motif of the harp itself, played by a king, is a familiar and powerful one, of course. The biblical King David is often depicted in illuminated manuscripts as playing a harp, though to be more historically accurate it should really be a type of lyre; according to legend, Alfred the Great disguised himself as a minstrel-harper and entered the camp of the chieftain Guthrum in order to spy on his Danish enemies. A harp alleged to be that of the famous 'first king of all Ireland', the chieftain Brian Boru, who united the tribes against the Viking onslaught in the tenth century, is preserved in Trinity College Dublin, and became the symbol for Ireland and all things Irish, representing the island on the Royal Standard of 1603, and on Guinness bottles and beer mats in more recent times.

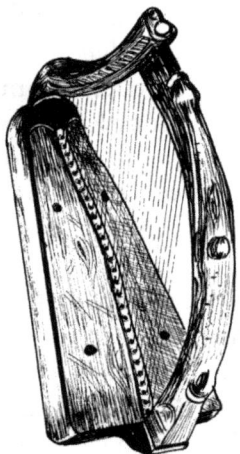

Brian Boru's Harp

The mention of the hart, a male deer, also has connotations of magic and crossing 'between the worlds'. A white hart is frequently the mystical sign that appears before Arthur and his knights as an indication that they are about to embark on a quest. In Celtic mythology particularly, the white hart is a harbinger of doom, and it is considered extremely unlucky to kill one. In the legend of Herne the Hunter, King Richard II is saved from such a beast in the forest of Windsor, but the hunter himself ultimately meets a tragic death, and, according to Shakespeare,

King Orfeo

his ghost is condemned to haunt a great oak where he 'blasts the tree, and takes the cattle, and makes milch-kine [milk-cows] yield blood'. Richard II adopted the white hart as his heraldic badge, and it has appeared on countles inn signs ever since.

White Hart depicted on the Wilton diptych *(c.* 1395)

The white hart was usually considered impossible to hunt down, and perhaps for this reason it came to symbolize man's never-ending quest for knowledge. Deer bones and antlers are often found as part of ritual deposits at ancient sacred sites — perhaps the line 'where the hart goes yearly' contains a faint memory of annual sacrificial rites, carried out in 'the woods so early'. This line is a translation from the Shetlandic 'Norn' dialect (*Whar giorten han grün oarlac*) in the Child ballad. The word 'oarlac' is very close to 'aurochs', the enormous wild cattle depicted in ochre and charcoal drawings found on the walls of cave galleries such as those at Lascaux in France, and Altamira in Spain, and which are supposed to have died out in Britain in the Iron Age, though they still lingered on in medieval Europe. In 1999 the horns and part of the skull of an aurochs were found in a dig in Fengate,

Songs from the Magical Tradition

Peterborough, and the remains are believed to have been used for ceremony or ritual.

The song was recorded by Caitlin Matthews and Bob Stewart for their album *Deep Well in the Wildwood*. Frankie Armstrong sang a longer, reconstructed version on her 1996 album *Till the Grass O'ergrew the Corn*. The sleeve notes commented: 'Brian Pearson thought that there were too few ballads about musicians to let this one disappear altogether, and rebuilt the text into the sort of shape it might have had before its almost terminal battering by time. The sprightly tune is that collected from John Stickle of Baltasound, Unst by Pat Shuldham-Shaw in 1947.' This version is certainly a very skillful re-imagining of how the ballad, in a more complete form, may have once sounded, though in this case the king plays the pipes, rather than a harp, while oddly the 'hart' line is dropped in favour of 'Where the green leaves they grow rarely'.

The ballad 'King Orfeo' is a fascinating synthesis of Classical mystery religion and revenant Celtic mysticism, whose author must certainly have been familiar with both traditions. It has also somehow managed to survive relatively unscathed from a time when all forms of paganism were proscribed by the Church, significantly before the study of pagan philosophy, culture and literature came to be tolerated in the European Renaissance of the fourteenth to seventeenth centuries. Perhaps it is even more surprising that the ballad survived for so long in the oral folk tradition of Shetland, but we must be very grateful that it has endured 'time's battering', as it is one of the brightest gems in the magical tradition.

music page 136

11. Lady Margaret

Lady Margaret she sits on a fine feather bed
O'er the midnight hour coming on,
A ghostly figure came to her room
And unto her did appear, appear,
And unto her did appear.

'Are you my father the King she said?
Or are you my brother John?
Or are you by chance my own true love
This night from Scotland along, along?
This night from Scotland along.'

'Well I'm not your father the King he said
Nor am I your brother John,
But I'm bechance your own true love
This night from Scotland along, along,
This night from Scotland along.'

'Lady Margaret, Lady Margaret' he cried
'Oh for love or charity,
Will you give to me my plighted troth
That once, love I gave thee, gave thee,
That once, love I gave thee.'

'Oh I'll not give you your plighted troth
Nor any such a thing,
Till you take me unto my father's hall
Where oft-times we have been, a been,
Where oft-times we have been.'

Well he took her then to her father's hall
And as they entered in,
The gates flew open of their own free will
Oh to let young William in, oh in
To let young William in.

'Oh Margaret, Oh Margaret' he cried
'Oh for love or charity,
Will you give to me my treasured troth
That once, love I gave thee, gave thee,
That once, love I gave thee.'

'Well I'll not give you your treasured troth
Nor any such a thing,
Till you take me unto yon churchyard
And marry me with a ring, a ring,
And marry me with a ring.'

Well he took her then to yon churchyard
And as they entered in,
The gates flew open of their own free will
For to let young William in, oh in,
To let young William in.

'And Margaret, Lady Margaret' he cried
'Oh for love or charity,
Will you give to me my plighted troth
That once, love I gave thee, gave thee,
That once, love I gave thee.'

Well out of her pocket she drew a cross
And she placed upon his breast,

Lady Margaret

'Here me love, the plighted troth
And heaven may your soul have rest, have rest,
And heaven may your soul have rest.'

'For the winds do blow and the moorcock do crow
And it's nearly breaking day,
It's time for the living to part from the dead
For now my love I'm away, away,
Now, my love I'm away'

This song is a variant of 'Sweet William's Ghost', which appears in Francis James Child's collection (#77), in the version that was included in Ramsay's *Tea Table Miscellany* of 1740. In the fullest version of the story the dead lover comes back to his mistress to ask for the return of his unfulfilled troth-plight. Not knowing that he is dead, she demands that he must first come to her bower and kiss her. The ghost replies that if he does so, her days 'will not be long'. She then refuses to return the troth until they are married in church. From there the ballad versions differ greatly. Sometimes the troth is returned, but only after the ghost admits he is dead. In some versions she follows the ghost to his grave and asks if there is room in it for her, and is told there is not. Usually Margaret will not give William back his troth until he has answered certain questions about death and the afterlife, such as 'where the children go that die without a name', or 'where the women go that hang themsell for sin', or that 'die in child beddin.' Child points out that while 'mere curiosity does not sort well with this very serious ballad [...] the scene at the grave may be judged grotesque, but it is not trivial or unimpressive'.

The lyrics printed above are taken from the singing of James Findlay, on his debut album *As I Carelessly Did Stray*, who learned it from Paddy Tunny's recording of 1975. In the song Margaret dispatches the reluctant ghost with a cross, rather than returning the troth. There is almost an element of trickery involved here, as it dawns on her, perhaps because of the supernatural opening of

Songs from the Magical Tradition

Red Grouse — old engraving (1859)

the gates, that this is not her 'young William', but an apparition, or perhaps she realized he was a ghost all along and carried the cross 'with malice aforethought', as it were, as presenting a cross was believed to be effective for laying a ghost or spirit from the otherworld — a trope familiar nowadays from many vampire movies. Incidentally, a 'moorcock' is a male red grouse, and grouse are regarded to be spirit messengers in many cultures across the world including the Americas, northern Europe and Central Asia. The crowing of the Moorcock presages daybreak, and illustrates the age-old belief that ghosts must retreat from the world of the living at dawn, yet another motif 'borrowed' by the creators of Gothic horror stories and films. The song also illustrates the belief that the dead cannot rest in peace leaving behind an unfulfilled commitment.

The song is related to several other songs in Francis Child's collection, 'Fair Margaret and Sweet William' being the obvious one, and there are clear parallels with 'The Unquiet Grave'. In one version at least, Lady Margaret's betrothed turns out to be Clerk Saunders, though this may have been through the influence of Walter Scott, who according to Child 'annexed' the ballad 'Sweet William's Ghost' in order to provide a more satisfactory ending for

Lady Margaret

his version of the 'Clerk Saunders' ballad in his book *Minstrelsy of the Scottish Borders* (1802). Child also found parallels with several Danish and German ballads, in most of which versions the woman dies at the ghost's grave. The song 'Willy-O', also known as 'Bay of Biscay', in which the ghost's body lies in the West Indies is probably a nineteenth-century re-write and was popular in Ireland.

The presentation of a betrothal ring or other token was a very serious affair, especially if the man were to be away for some time, on a journey perhaps, or at war. Effectively it was a contract, and not to be broken lightly, and was probably derived from handfastings in medieval times. The engagement ring is, of course, the modern equivalent. Often the troth was broken in two, each of the partners keeping one half. This was especially the case if the betrothal token was a coin, but rings were also broken as this example from around 1780, published in *The Exeter Garland* illustrates:

> A ring of pure gold she from her finger took,
> And just in the middle the same then she broke.
> Quoth she 'as a token of love you this take
> And this as a pledge I will keep for your sake.'

'Gimmel rings' of gold or silver were popular throughout Europe. These were of two or three parts (two for the couple, the third for a witness) that could be brought together and riveted into one for the wedding ceremony, as illustrated by this passage from John Dryden's *Don Sebastian* (1690).

> A curious artist wrought them,
> With joints so close, as not to be perceiv'd;
> Yet are they both each other's counterpart, and in the midst,
> A heart divided in two halves was plac'd.

The custom also appears frequently in Shakespeare's work, in this example from *Measure for Measure* (c.1604) Marianna's betrothed lover, the scoundrel Angelo, breaks the contract after the accidental loss of her dowry at sea:

Left her in her tears, and dried not one of them with his comfort; swallowed his vows whole, pretending in her discoveries of dishonour: in few, bestowed her on her own lamentation, which she yet wears for his sake; and he, a marble to her tears, is washed with them, but relents not.

Gimmel Rings — **engraving published 1912**

The oath 'by my troth' is also used frequently by Shakespeare's characters, emphasizing, perhaps, the importance of the rite in seventeenth-century England at least.

When death intervened to break a betrothal, as in 'Sweet William's Ghost', superstitions were, understandably, rife. Walter Scott's poem *Advertisement of a Pirate* tells of a lady who went up to see her dying lover: 'arriving too late she had the courage to request a sight of his body; and then touching the hand of the corpse, she formally resumed the troth-plight which she had bestowed'. Scott informs us that 'she could not, according to the superstition of the country, have escaped a visit from the ghost of her departed lover, in the event of her bestowing on any living suitor the faith which she had plighted to the dead'. This was apparently related to him by an old woman in Shetland. Presumably Lady Margaret was not aware of this superstition, or she may have been more willing to return William's troth!

music page 137

12. The Lambton Worm

One Sunday morn young Lambton went a-fishing' in the Wear;
An' catched a fish upon he's heuk, he thowt leuk't varry queer.
But whatt'n a kind of fish it was young Lambton cuddent tell.
He waddn't fash te carry'd hyem, so he hoyed it doon a well.

Whisht! Lads, haad yor gobs,
An Aa'll tell ye's aall an aaful story
Whisht! Lads, haad yor gobs,
An' Aa'll tell ye 'boot the worm.

Noo Lambton felt inclined te gan an' fight i' foreign wars.
He joined a troop o' Knights that cared for nowther woonds nor scars,
An' off he went te Palestine where queer things him befel,
An' varry seun forgat aboot the queer worm i' the well.

Whisht! Lads ...

But the worm got fat an' growed and' growed an' growed an aaful size;
He'd greet big teeth, a greet big gob, an' greet big goggle eyes.
An' when at neets he craaled aboot te pick up bits o' news,
If he felt dry upon the road, he milked a dozen coos.

Whisht! Lads ...

This feorful worm wad often feed on caalves an' lambs an' sheep,
An' swally little barins alive when they laid doon te sleep.
An' when he'd eaten aall he cud an' he had had he's fill,
He craaled away an' lapped he's tail seven times roond Pensher Hill.

Songs from the Magical Tradition

Whisht! Lads ...

The news of this myest aaful worm an' his queer gannins on
Seun crossed the seas, gat te the ears ov brave and' bowld Sor John.
So hyem he cam an' catched the beast an' cut 'im in twe haalves,
An' that seun stopped he's eatin' bairns, an' sheep an' lambs an' caalves.

Whisht! Lads ...

So noo ye knaa hoo aall the foaks on byeth sides ov the Wear
Lost lots o' sheep an' lots o' sleep an' leeved i' mortal feor.
So let's hev one te brave Sor John that kept the bairns frae harm,
Saved coos an' caalves by myekin' halves o' the famis Lambton Worm.

Noo lads, Aa'll haad me gob,
That's aall Aa knaa aboot the story
Ov Sor John's clivvor job
Wi' the aaful Lambton Worm.

A version of one of England's most enduring folk tales about a dragon, this song is known from two versions published in the Victorian era. The jocular dialect song appeared in 1867, in Tait's *Edinburgh Magazine* and soon became a firm music-hall favourite, while a much more extensive ballad version with a somewhat moralizing tone was published by Revd J. Watson in *The Local Historian's Table-book* (1875). There were certainly earlier versions as it is referred to as an old ballad in Sir Cuthbert Sharpe's *The Bishoprick Garland* (1834), in which four verses are quoted.

The tale revolves around John Lambton, heir of the Lambton Estate on Wearside, and his battle with a giant worm, which had been terrorizing the local villages; 'worm', in this instance is a version of the Anglo-Saxon 'wyrm', meaning 'dragon', or 'serpent'. William Langland's *Piers Plowman* (fourteenth-century), speaks of 'wyld wormes in woods'; the word is also used in this sense in the famous ballad, 'The laidly Worm of Spindlestane Heughs'.

The story relates how the rebellious young John missed church one Sunday to fish in the River Wear. All he managed to catch that day was a small, strange eel-like creature with nine holes on each side

The Lambton Worm

***The "Laidly Worm" of London and Young County Council* (1890)
— here the *Punch* cartoonist has confused two quite different legends!**

of a salamander-like head. In different versions, it varies in size from no bigger than his thumb to about three feet long. John, in disgust, declared that he had caught the devil and threw his catch down a nearby well. He then forgot all about it, and later, as penance for his rebellious youth, he went off to fight in the crusades.

Eventually, the well became poisonous as the worm grew and grew. The villagers' livestock started to disappear and it soon transpired that the worm had emerged fully grown from the well and taken up residence at a local hill, around which it coiled itself. The worm terrorized the villagers, eating their sheep, drinking a whole herds-worth of cows' milk and snatching away small children. It would then head off to Lambton Castle, where the lord managed to appease the creature with a daily ritual offering of the milk of nine good cows, twenty gallons, or a full wooden/stone trough-full, depending on which version you hear. A number of brave villagers tried to kill the beast but were quickly dispatched. Even when the worm was cut into sections, it simply reassembled itself. Visiting knights had no greater success than the villagers and none survived the encounter.

Eventually, after seven years, John Lambton returned from the crusades to find his father's estate almost destitute because of the worm. He resolved to fight it, but first, he wisely sought advice from a witch near Durham. She told him to cover his armour in metal spikes or blades and fight the worm in the deepest, fastest flowing part of the river, so that the pieces would be swept away by the current and could not re-attach. The witch demanded that, in return for her services, he must slay the first living thing he sees after killing the worm, or his family will be cursed for nine generations and none will die naturally in their beds.

Aware of the curse, John arranged to sound his hunting horn three times once the beast was dead, on which signal his father was to release a hound which John would kill. The witch's advice proved sound — the worm died, unable to heal itself, and John sounded his horn. Unfortunately, in his excitement, his father forgot to release the hound and rushed to congratulate his son. John could not bear to kill his father and so nine generations of Lambtons were cursed.

A splendid story. One which contains many motifs of English mythology and folklore. It is relatively unusual, however, to be able to trace both the actual places in which the tale took place, and the main character in the story, for the legend, while obviously apocryphal, is based on a real person, Sir John Lambton, of whom an old manuscript states 'John Lambeton that slew ye Worme was knight of Rhodes'. The Knights of St John of Rhodes were a band of Christian warriors with whom John was active in the Holy Land in the fourteenth century.

The curse seems to have held true for at least three generations, possibly helping to contribute to the popularity of the story: in the first generation, Robert Lambton died of drowning at Newrig, in the second, Colonel William Lambton was killed at Marston Moor, and in the third a William Lambton died in battle at Wakefield; in the ninth generation, Henry Lambton died in his

The Lambton Worm

carriage as it crossed the bridge at Lambton on 26 June 1761. It must be assumed that the curse died with him — his brother, though he understandably had lived in fear of a violent death, died in his bed at a great old age.

Worm Hill is on the north bank of the Wear, just over a mile from Lambton Hall. It is a low mound, possibly artificial, and there was once a Worm Rock, which was said to have acted as a trough from which the worm was said to have consumed its daily offering. Worm Well was also supposed to be nearby, but only the hill appears on the 1857 Ordnance Survey map, and both well and rock are absent today. An alternative to Worm Hill, which is mentioned in the song, is Penshaw hill, actually an Iron Age hill-fort, the only one in the North East to have triple ramparts — said, of course, to be the marks of the worm's coiled body where it slept. J.S. Moore, in *The Pictorial Book of Ballads* (1849) conjectures that the legend may have

> arisen from the circumstance of an invasion from a foreign foe, some successful chieftain, with well-disciplined bands, destroying and laying waste with fire and sword, whose advance over unequal ground would convey to the fears of the peasantry the appearance of a rolling serpent; and the power of re-uniting is readily accounted for by the ordinary evolutions of military tactics. And by the knight's destroying this legion by his single arm, is supposed to be signified that he was the head and chief in the onslaught.

It is always tempting to read remnants of ancient pagan belief in a story such as the Lambton Worm. Worm hill, may well have been a ritual monument, and the sufferings of the villagers may have been due to a priest demanding ever more extravagant offerings to a pagan deity, represented by a serpent, or worm, dispatched by a saintly warrior, who had done penance in the Holy Land for a former life of debauchery. However, this would put even more of a Christian spin on the story than the Victorian ballads do. While some such motifs in folklore may have their origins in the symbolic battle between indigenous paganism and early Christianity, here it may be safer simply to treat the tale as a great yarn, probably concocted in the Early Modern period as a kind of morality tale to explain the unusual misfortune of at least three generations of Lambtons. Nevertheless, its symbolism is intriguing.

Illustration from a theatre programme (1860s)

Pantomime versions of the story have often been performed, notably at the Tyne Theatre in Newcastle in 1867, and there is even an opera in two acts by composer Robert Sherlaw Johnson, first performed in 1978. The song has been recorded many times, perhaps most famously by Brian Ferry and Roxy Music, while a version of it ('The D'Ampton Worm') accompanies one of the opening scenes of Ken Russell's deliriously silly film *The Lair of the White Worm*. The film is loosely based on the story by Bram Stoker, which clearly borrows from the Lambton legend. A statue of Sir John, in his spiked armour, which according to Walker is 'evidently of great antiquity', stands in Lambton Hall, and the legend is also the subject of a public sculpture by Craig Knowles in Elba Park, Houghton-le-Spring, Sunderland.

music page 138

13. The Somerset Wassail

Wassail and Wassail all over the town!
The cup it is white and the ale it is brown;
The cup it is made of the good ashen tree,
And so is the malt of the best barley:

For it's your wassail, and it's our wassail!
And it's joy be to you, and jolly wassail!

O master and missus, are you all within?
Pray open the door and let us come in;
O master and missus sitting by the fire,
Pray think upon poor travellers, a-travelling in the mire.

For it's your wassail ...

O where is the maid, with the silver-headed pin,
To open the door, and let us come in?
O master and missus, it is our desire
A good loaf and cheese, and a toast by the fire.

For it's your wassail ...

There was an old man, and he had an old cow,
And how for to keep her he didn't know how,
He built up a barn for to keep his cow warm,
And a drop or two of cider won't do us no harm:

Songs from the Magical Tradition

No harm, boys, harm; no harm, boys, harm;
And a drop or two of cider will do us no harm.

The girt dog of Langport he burnt his long tail,
And this is the night we go singing wassail:
O master and missus, now we must be gone;
God bless all in this house till we do come again.

The Anglo-Saxons used the phrase *wæs hal!* as an everyday greeting. *Wæs* is a form of the verb to 'be', related to modern English 'was'; *hal* is the ancestor of the modern English words whole and hale. Thus, *wæs hal!* literally meant 'be healthy!'. The Vikings who later settled in Northern England used a dialectal variant of the same phrase: *Ves heill!* Since the Anglo-Saxons and Norse shared a custom of welcoming guests by presenting them with a horn of ale (or cup of mead, or goblet of wine), the greeting evolved into a toast. The phrase was eventually contracted into one word, wassail, and came to refer to the act of toasting someone's health — wassailing, and to a type of alcoholic beverage (spiced ale, cider or punch) used to toast people's health on special occasions. Wassail became synonymous with good cheer: in *Beowulf* the 'warriors' wassail and words of power, the proud band's revel' are described as an important, life-affirming part of the ritual of everyday life in the 'festal hall'. Based on this evidence alone, the wassailing tradition pre-dates the Norman Conquest and may be well over a thousand years old. The following is an excerpt from Ronald Hutton's *Stations of the Sun*:

> In Southern England a set of customs was grouped under the name of wassailing. They consisted, in essence, of wishing health to crops and animals much as people passing the wassail bowl wished it to each other. Most are well recorded in the early modern period, and they may quite easily have descended directly from pagan practices, although it is also possible that they developed outwards from the domestic wassail. The most widespread, famous, and enduring concerned fruit trees. It is first mentioned at Fordwich, Kent, in 1585, by which time it was already in part the preserve of groups of young men who went between orchards

performing the rite for a reward. Robert Herrick, almost certainly writing about Devon and in the 1630s, spoke of 'wassailing' the fruit-bearing trees in order to assure good yields, and in the 1660s and 1670s a Sussex clergyman gave money to boys who came to 'howl' his orchard (being the enduring local term). John Aubrey, describing West Country customs in the same period, said that on Twelfth Eve men 'go with their wassel-bowl into the orchard and go about the trees to bless them, and put a piece of toast upon the roots, in order to do it'.

***The Wassail Bowl*, by George Gilbert (1860)**

The use of wassailing to mean 'carolling' (as in 'Here we go a-wassailing') stems from the custom of singing songs whilst drinking from the 'wassail cup' during Christmas and New Year celebrations, for rewards of food, drink or money. Such survivals are probably relics of the feudal system in the Middle Ages, in which there was a symbiotic relationship between the peasantry and their feudal overlords. On certain occasions, the 'common folk' would initiate a form of charitable giving from the lord and lady of the manor, in which music, song and dance often played

Songs from the Magical Tradition

an important part of the proceedings. Such ritual almsgiving was played out at several important dates in the year, and no doubt to some degree helped to maintain the status quo, and subvert any underlying hostility felt by the oppressed peasant towards his masters. The Church sometimes played a part, as in the Whitsuntide 'church ales' or the feasting at Martinmas which provided food and good cheer to the poor. However, the Church itself took a long time to come to terms with a 'Christmas season', and many of the midwinter customs that thrived in the Middle Ages and after were of a secular nature, carolling being one of them. It is in this context that the sixteenth-century carol 'We Wish you a Merry Christmas', with its elements of propitiating neighbours for 'figgy pudding' etc should be seen.

The 'Wassail cup' or bowl was of some importance as a ritual object in its own right, and according to different traditions, as specified in song lyrics was usually made either of ash, maple, or elder. It would have been used ceremonially both at 'visiting' and 'orchard wassails', in many cases bedecked with ribbons for the occasion, and also for other feasts during the midwinter season. A drink known as 'lambs' wool' was traditional fare for the wassail cup, which consisted of mulled ale, beaten eggs, sugar, spices (usually nutmeg, cloves and ginger) and roasted apples. The line in Shakespeare's *Loves Labours Lost* (Act 5 scene 2) 'When roasted crabs hiss in the bowl', refers to small apples which burst open when roasted, to provide the soft white 'lambs' wool' of the traditional wassail drink. The concoction would be drunk with each member of the assembled company shouting in turn 'Waes Hael!', to which the response from the others would be 'Drink Hael!'

The 'visiting wassail' tradition was fairly straightforward: a group of people would meet on the evening of the appointed day and visit households in the neighbourhood, either where they knew they would be received favourably, or where a prior arrangement had been made. The principle purpose of the custom was to wish good health to the householders by singing the wassailing song,

The Somerset Wassail

for which rewards were expected — usually in the form of liquid or other refreshment. An important facet of the tradition was that those involved were not to be confused with, or regarded as, common beggars: in Somerset, and elsewhere, it was forbidden for the wassailers to actually knock on the door; those who sang 'Here we come a wassailing' would assure the lord and lady of the manor that 'we are not daily beggars that beg from door to door but we are friendly neighbours, whom you have seen before'. After they had been plied with food and drink, they would respond:

> Love and joy come to you,
> And to you your wassail too;
> And God bless you and send you a Happy New Year.

A notable part of the Somerset tradition is that after completing their accustomed route, the assembled company would adjourn to the local inn, where the 'ashen faggot' was ritually laid in the hearth. This was a large bundle of ash logs, up to a yard or so long, bound with up to fifteen bonds of withy or hazel in multiples of three. As each bond broke, the wassailers would drink a toast, in some cases a whole pint pot of cider for each bond — so an evening of joyous conviviality was assured! An odd addenda to the custom at Roadwater, on Exmoor, had the wassailers entering the local inn by the back door and leaving by the front, after drinking a toast to the landlord. A reversal of this manner of entry and exit would, it was said, bring very bad luck to the inn.

The clergyman and sensualist poet Robert Herrick (1591-1674) often celebrated English village life and rural traditions, and his poem *The Wassail* was probably written about the tradition as he experienced it in Devon, for he was vicar of Dean Prior, near Exeter, from 1629 to 1674. It contains an element of mild cursing towards those who fail to respond favourably to the wassailers:

> Give way, give way, ye gates, and win
> An easy blessing to your bin
> And basket, by our entering in.
>
> May both with manchet stand replete,
> Your larders, too, so hung with meat,
> That though a thousand thousand eat,

Songs from the Magical Tradition

Yet ere twelve moons shall whirl about
Their silvery spheres, there's none may doubt
But more's sent in than was served out.

Next, may your dairies prosper so
As that your pans no ebb may know;
But if they do, the more to flow,

Like to a solemn, sober stream,
Banked all with lilies, and the cream
Of sweetest cowslips filling them.

Then may your plants be pressed with fruit,
Nor bee or hive you have be mute,
But sweetly sounding like a lute.

Last, may your harrows, shares, and ploughs,
Your stacks, your stocks, your sweetest mows,
All prosper by your virgin vows.

Alas! we bless, but see none here,
That brings us either ale or beer;
In a dry house all things are near.

Let's leave a longer time to wait,
Where rust and cobwebs bind the gate;
And all live here with needy fate;

Where chimneys do forever weep
For want of warmth, and stomachs keep
With noise the servants' eyes from sleep.

It is in vain to sing or stay
Our free feet here, but we'll away;
Yet to the Lares this we'll say:

The time will come when you'll be sad,
And reckon this for fortune bad,
T' have lost the good ye might have had.

With the decline in agriculture and the consequent widespread movement of rural populations into industrial towns in the nineteenth century, such customs migrated to an urban environment with a less rigid, hierarchical structure. Perhaps inevitably, wassailing and carolling sometimes degenerated into door-to-door begging, often with menaces, a little like the modern-day 'trick or treating' at Halloween, and a once proud

The Somerset Wassail

and popular tradition came to be seen as nothing more than an excuse for drunkenness and rowdy behaviour.

Probably more ancient is the tradition of wassailing apple orchards: each year around Old Christmas Eve (5 January) or Old Twelfth Night (17 January) the people of Somerset, Devon, Worcestershire, Sussex and Kent, the principle cider making areas of England, would all wassail their apple trees to ensure a fine crop of cider apples in the summer ahead. The actual date is not particularly important, possibly because of the confusion surrounding the 'old and new style' calendars, and nowadays the ceremonies are usually held during a weekend between these two dates. What is important is that the wassail takes place after dusk around the darkest time of the year. In Worcestershire, there was an association of wassailing with fire ritual — here men would light 'twelfth-night bonfires' in the fields in order to protect the following year's wheat crop as a prelude to wassailing the orchards. Perhaps the Somerset custom of lighting the ashen faggot was a more domesticated form of this tradition.

Traditionally the wassail ceremony involved farm-workers visiting the orchard after dark with shotguns, horns, food and a large pail or bowl of cider — the wassail cup, or bowl. The celebrants would approach the trees with burning torches, and sometimes the orchard would be lit up with a bonfire. Often a processional tune or song was used to approach each orchard in turn. Usually the best tree would be selected to represent the whole plantation, and this is sometimes referred to as the 'Apple Tree Man'. A libation of cider, usually hot and spiced, would be poured over its roots and pieces of toast, or cakes soaked in cider would be placed in the forks of branches, or impaled on twigs; one ceremony in Devon involved hoisting a young boy into the branches, who, representing the spirit of the tree, would be propitiated with gifts of bread, cheese and cider. In a few cases a 'Wassail King and Queen' would be chosen to preside over the ceremony. The wassail song would be sung or chanted as a

Songs from the Magical Tradition

blessing or charm to bring fruitfulness, or even in admonishment not to fail in the coming year. Sometimes the tree would be given a clue to what was expected of it: men would circle the trunk bowed down as if under a heavy weight of harvested apples. The assembled company would drink from the wassail bowl and toast the tree loudly and merrily. Shotguns were fired, horns blown and pots and pans beaten randomly, to scare off malevolent spirits and awaken the tree from its winter slumber. A correspondent writing in the *Gentleman's Magazine* in 1791 notes a curious custom observed after the apple wassailing in Devon:

> In the south hams [villages] of Devonshire, on the eve of the Epiphany, the farmer, attended by his workmen, with a large pitcher of cider, goes to the orchard, and there encircling one of the best bearing trees they drink the following toast three several times:

> Here's to thee, old apple-tree,
> Whence thou mayst bud, and whence thou mayst blow!
> And whence thou mayst bear apples enow!
> Hats full! Caps full!
> Bushel-bushel-sacks full,
> And my pockets full too! Huzza!

> This done, they return to the house, the doors of which they are sure to find bolted by the females, who, be the weather what it may, are inexorable to all entreaties to open them till some one has guessed at what is on the spit, which is generally some nice little thing, difficult to hit on, and is their reward of him who first names it. The doors are then thrown open, and the lucky clod pole receives the tit-bit as his recompense. Some are not so superstitious as to believe that if they neglect this custom the trees will bear no apples that year.

For apple tree wassailing the traditional chant, or toast was more important than the song. Other chants that have survived to be recorded include the following:

> Huzza, Huzza, in our good town
> The bread shall be white, and the liquor be brown
> So here my old fellow I drink to thee

The Somerset Wassail

And the very health of each other tree.
Well may ye blow, well may ye bear
Blossom and fruit both apple and pear.
So that every bough and every twig
May bend with a burden both fair and big
May ye bear us and yield us fruit such a store
That the bags and chambers and house run o'er.
[Cornworthy, Devon, 1805]

Apple tree, apple tree, we all come to wassail thee,
Bear this year and next year to bloom and to blow,
Hat fulls, cap fulls, three-cornered sack fulls,
Hip, Hip, Hip, hurrah,
Holler boys, holler hurrah.'
[Street, Somerset, 1909]

Apple-tree, apple-tree,
Bear good fruit,
Or down with your top
And up with your root.
[South Hams, Devon, 19th century]

Bud well, bear well
God send you fare well;
Every sprig and every spray
A bushel of apples next New Year Day.
[Worcestershire, 19th century]

In Sussex wassailers were frequently known as 'howlers', or 'the howling boys', presumably because of the racket they customarily made, and a captain and vice-captain oversaw the proceedings. An 1897 photograph shows them at Duncton dressed in bright floral robes, with apples hung around their necks and on their hats. A large cow horn was used to serenade the trees, which were also beaten with sticks. After 'howling' the orchards, a 'visiting wassail' was then carried out around the village, ending up in the Cricketers Inn. Interestingly, there seems also to have been a custom of 'howling' beehives in Sussex, as mentioned by T. W. Horsefield in 1827 (it seems to have died out not long afterwards). Quite how this was achieved is unfortunately not recorded.

Songs from the Magical Tradition

> Here's to thee, old apple tree.
> Stand fast root; bear well top.
> Every twig, apples big.
> Every bough, apples enou'.
> Hats full, caps full, four and twenty sacks full.
> [Sussex, 19th century]

The Somerset Wassail was noted down by the great folk song collector Cecil Sharp from a performance of the Drayton Wassailers some time before the First World War. Drayton is a hamlet on Sedgemoor just south of Langport. Like many traditional songs that stem from a ritual tradition, its lyrics have elements of nonsense, supplication and celebration. A large number of broadly similar songs have been collected from Cornwall to Yorkshire, and many enshrine an element of local folklore — in this case the reference to a 'girt dog of Langport' which bears further examination.

Black dog legends are rife in the West Country, though none appear to have survived in the vicinity of Langport. However, a ghostly 'gurt dog', in this case a benevolent apparition, is said to haunt the Quantock Hills some way to the west. Avalonian questers connect the 'Girt Dog' with the 'Glastonbury Zodiac', an alleged astrologically configured landscape feature with the zodiacal signs formed by hills, roads and rivers. Katherine Maltwood who 'discovered' it in the 1930s, claimed it represented the original Round Table of Avalon, with Arthur, Guinevere, Merlin and the chief knights seated around it as the signs of the Zodiac and the seasons of the year. She referred to a great hound five miles long as the Girt Dog of Langport, which was her 'star temple's' guardian. Maltwood wrote two books — *Glastonbury's Temple of the Stars* and *The Enchantments of Britain*. It is quite likely that she came across the line when the song was first published in 1928 in the *Oxford Book of Carols*, as this was around the time she was researching her theories, and decided that the 'girt dog' would be a suitable name for her astrological guardian.

A plausible reason for the inclusion of the 'girt dog' in the song, and one that Cecil Sharp proposed, is that it may be a reference to the

The Somerset Wassail

Wassailing in Somerset 2012 (photo: James Findlay)

sacking of Langport by the Danes, whose invasion is still remembered in that town, so close to the Somerset levels that were the refuge of Alfred the Great during his exile in the ninth century. The invading Danes were often referred to as wolves by the Anglo-Saxons and the reference to a 'girt dog' (great wolf) of Langport getting his tail burned might be a reference to Alfred's eventual expulsion of the Danes from his kingdom of Wessex. Another intriguing but remote possibility is that the 'girt dog' getting his tail burned might refer to an earlier battle fought in the year 509 between the Saxons of Wessex and the Celtic Dumnonians who controlled the land to the west. There was also the Battle of Langport in the English Civil War in 1645 when the royalists under Lord George Goring were heavily defeated by Fairfax's New Model Army on their way to relieve the siege of Taunton. Perhaps a Civil War scholar might be able to find some relevance to the 'girt dog of Langport' in this context.

The oldest claimed unbroken tradition of orchard wassailing is at the Butchers Arms at Carhampton in Somerset, which is held on 17 January each year, but with the growing popularity of morris dancing, which has attached itself to the wassailing tradition over the years, wassails are now held throughout the country and the Somerset Wassail song may be heard in many places at this time of year.

The wassail tradition is one of our oldest, and most comprehensively recorded seasonal traditions, and it is one which anyone can enjoy, with friends, or with a small family gathering — if you happen to have an apple tree in the garden that is, or by joining in one of the many public ceremonies now held around the country, usually hosted by morris sides, which often have a strong Pagan following. One of the most popular wassails is now held every year at Middle Farm, Firle, East Sussex, and is organized by the Pagan border morris side Hunters Moon. At the time of writing, the wassail chant used for the ceremony is a self-consciously Pagan offering penned a few years ago by the author of this book, with the idea of encouraging today's Druids, Wiccans and other Pagans to re-create, and participate in one of our most ancient seasonal customs:

> Oh apple tree we honour thee
> In hope that you will bear
> The blessed fruit of Avalon
> At harvest time each year.
>
> Each golden apple you bring forth
> A gift to Aphrodite,
> Has at its heart a pentacle,
> The symbol of her mystery.
>
> Your blossom heralds Springtime
> Your leaf brings Summer shade.
> Let Samhain's harvest cup be filled
> With cider freshly made.
>
> When Winter's cold envelops you
> In wind and rain and hail
> Then we'll return each year to bring
> Our grateful thanks WASSAIL!

music page 139

14. Tam Lin

There's nane that gaes by Carterhaugh
But they leave him a wad,
Either their rings, or green mantles,
Or else their maidenhead.

Janet has kilted her green kirtle
A little aboon her knee,
And she has broded her yellow hair
A little aboon her bree,
And she's awa to Carterhaugh
As fast as she can hie.

When she came to Carterhaugh
Tam Lin was at the well,
And there she fand his steed standing,
But away was himsel.

She had na pu'd a double rose,
A rose but only twa,
Till upon then started young Tam Lin,
Says, Lady, thou's pu nae mae.
Why pu's thou the rose, Janet,
And why breaks thou the wand?
Or why comes thou to Carterhaugh
Withoutten my command?

"Carterhaugh, it is my own,
My daddy gave it me,
I'll come and gang by Carterhaugh,
And ask nae leave at thee."
Janet has kilted her green kirtle
A little aboon her knee,
And she has broded her yellow hair
A little aboon her bree,
And she is to her father's ha,
As fast as she can hie.
Four and twenty ladies fair
Were playing at the ba,
And out then came the fair Janet,
The flower among them a'.
Four and twenty ladies fair
Were playing at the chess,
And out then came the fair Janet,
As green as onie glass.
Out then spake an auld grey knight,
Lay oer the castle wa,
And says, Alas, fair Janet, for thee,
But we'll be blamed a'.
"Haud your tongue, ye auld fac'd knight,
Some ill death may ye die!
Father my bairn on whom I will,
I'll father none on thee."
Out then spak her father dear,
And he spak meek and mild,
"And ever alas, sweet Janet," he says,
"I think thou gaest wi child."
"If that I gae wi child, father,
Mysel maun bear the blame,
There's neer a laird about your ha,
Shall get the bairn's name.

Tam Lin

"If my love were an earthly knight,
As he's an elfin grey,
I wad na gie my ain true-love
For nae lord that ye hae.
"The steed that my true love rides on
Is lighter than the wind,
Wi siller he is shod before,
Wi burning gowd behind."
Janet has kilted her green kirtle
A little aboon her knee,
And she has broded her yellow hair
A little aboon her bree,
And she's awa to Carterhaugh
As fast as she can hie.
When she came to Carterhaugh,
Tam Lin was at the well,
And there she fand his steed standing,
But away was himsel.
She had na pu'd a double rose,
A rose but only twa,
Till up then started young Tam Lin,
Says, Lady, thou pu's nae mae.
"Why pu's thou the rose, Janet,
Amang the groves sae green,
And a' to kill the bonny babe
That we gat us between?"
"O tell me, tell me, Tam Lin," she says,
"For's sake that died on tree,
If eer ye was in holy chapel,
Or christendom did see?"
"Roxbrugh he was my grandfather,
Took me with him to bide
And ance it fell upon a day
That wae did me betide.

Songs from the Magical Tradition

"And ance it fell upon a day
A cauld day and a snell,
When we were frae the hunting come,
That frae my horse I fell,
The Queen o' Fairies she caught me,
In yon green hill do dwell.

"And pleasant is the fairy land,
But, an eerie tale to tell,
Ay at the end of seven years,
We pay a tiend to hell,
I am sae fair and fu o flesh,
I'm feard it be mysel.

"But the night is Halloween, lady,
The morn is Hallowday,
Then win me, win me, an ye will,
For weel I wat ye may.

"Just at the mirk and midnight hour
The fairy folk will ride,
And they that wad their true-love win,
At Miles Cross they maun bide."

"But how shall I thee ken, Tam Lin,
Or how my true-love know,
Amang sa mony unco knights,
The like I never saw?"

"O first let pass the black, lady,
And syne let pass the brown,
But quickly run to the milk-white steed,
Pu ye his rider down.

"For I'll ride on the milk-white steed,
And ay nearest the town,
Because I was an earthly knight
They gie me that renown.

"My right hand will be gloved, lady,
My left hand will be bare,

Tam Lin

Cockt up shall my bonnet be,
And kaimed down shall my hair,
And thae's the takens I gie thee,
Nae doubt I will be there.

"They'll turn me in your arms, lady,
Into an esk and adder,
But hold me fast, and fear me not,
I am your bairn's father.

"They'll turn me to a bear sae grim,
And then a lion bold,
But hold me fast, and fear me not,
And ye shall love your child.

"Again they'll turn me in your arms
To a red het gand of airn,
But hold me fast, and fear me not,
I'll do you nae harm.

"And last they'll turn me in your arms
Into the burning gleed,
Then throw me into well water,
O throw me in with speed.

"And then I'll be your ain true-love,
I'll turn a naked knight,
Then cover me wi your green mantle,
And hide me out o sight."

Gloomy, gloomy was the night,
And eerie was the way,
As fair Jenny in her green mantle
To Miles Cross she did gae.

About the middle o the night
She heard the bridles sing,
This lady was as glad at that
As any earthly thing.

First she let the black pass by,
And syne she let the brown,

But quickly she ran to the milk-white steed,
And pu'd the rider down.

Sae weel she minded what he did say,
And young Tam Lin did win,
Syne coverd him wi her green mantle,
As blythe's a bird in spring

Out then spak the Queen o Fairies,
Out of a bush o broom,
"Them that has gotten young Tam Lin
Has gotten a stately-groom."

Out then spak the Queen o Fairies,
And an angry woman was she,
"Shame betide her ill-far'd face,
And an ill death may she die,
For she's taen awa the bonniest knight
In a' my companie.

"But had I kend, Tam Lin," she says,
"What now this night I see,
I wad hae taen out thy twa grey een,
And put in twa een o tree."

The above version is from Child's collection (#39), and is one of the earliest of no less than eleven complete ballad variants he quotes, along with several others in fragmentary form. The source is noted as 'Johnson's Museum (*Scot's Musical Museum* 1792). Communicated by Burns'. The story is plainly much older, as it is mentioned in Wedderburn's *Complaynt of Scotland* (1549).

The tale is one of the best-known in faerie lore, and as Katherine Briggs has noted, in its fuller versions, the ballad 'is a compendium of Scottish Fairy beliefs' containing as it does 'the carrying away of anyone who is unconscious of fairy ground, the transformations of mortals to fairies when they are kidnapped, the tiend [tithe] to Hell, the disenchantment through various

Tam Lin

transformations, finally confirmed by the putting on of a mortal garment'. In recent years many more versions have come to light, or been reconstructed from other fragments, and the ballad was brought to a wide audience by Fairport Convention, who recorded a version on their classic album *Liege and Lief* (1968). There is also a fine Scottish reel which bears the name 'Tam Lin' (see music page 142).

The woods of Carterhaugh (a real place near Selkirk on the Scottish Borders) have a fearful reputation as being guarded by Tam Lin, a man, or possibly a spirit, who demands a payment from all maidens who pass through, in the form of jewellery, clothing or even their virginity. A maiden named Janet ignores the warnings, and provocatively, she picks a rose in the woods while Tam Lin is otherwise engaged at a nearby well. He questions her right to pick the flowers, to which she replies that Carterhaugh is rightfully hers. She then returns to her father's house where, much to the concern of the household, she admits to being with child. She states that she alone is to blame, and that her lover is 'elfin'. She then sets off to find Tam Lin, and quizzes him about his

Illustration from *More English Fairy Tales* (1892)

origins. He is worried that she might be about to abort the child and admits to being a mortal — a nobleman who was captured by the Queen of the Faeries when he fell from his horse while out hunting; being the fairest man among them, he will soon be sacrificed to hell as part of a tithe that must be paid every seventh year. He then tells her how she can save him — she must wait at a crossroads on Halloween at midnight and pull him from his horse; she must then keep hold of him as he undergoes various transformations, before throwing him into a well when he turns into red hot iron. When he regains his own naked shape she must cover him with her green mantle and he will be hidden from the faeries' sight. This she does, much to the chagrin of the watching Elf Queen, for whom the young knight had been a highly prized prisoner, and a worthy tribute to the denizens of hell.

The story conforms quite well with the first of McKillop's hypotheses about the theoretical origins of faeries — that they are a folk-memory of a region's original inhabitants (see page 28) — an earlier race of beings somehow shifted by time to a supernatural dimension. To my mind quite the best, and most poetic, evocation of this, is expressed in the lyrics of the song 'Sideways to the Sun' by Horslips, on their album *Book of Invasions: A celtic Symphony* (1974):

> We're the mystery of the lake when the water's still.
> We're the laughter in the twilight
> You can hear behind the hill.
> We'll stay around to watch you laugh,
> Destroy yourselves for fun.
> But, you won't see us, we've grown sideways to the sun

The realm of faery is, significantly, once again represented in the ballad as being beneath a 'green hill'. The 'faerie hills', as ancient burial mounds were frequently referred to, are still regarded with a certain amount of awe, tinged with mysticism even today, often fenced in and heavily grazed or encroached upon by the plough, their surroundings despoiled by modern roads and farm buildings. Imagine how much stronger an impression they would have made centuries ago, when they were more numerous, and their settings unsullied by agriculture — the true abode of ancestral spirits. By extension, natural hills too, may be the abode of the elfin, and many have acquired the appellation 'barrow' over the years, such as Worbarrow and Bulbarrow in Dorset. James Walsh, the cunning man of Netherbury, who came before the authorities at Exeter in 1566 was described as communing with the fairies thus: 'He speaketh with them upon hyls, where as there is great heapes of earth, as namely in Dorsetshire.' There is a 'Barrow Hill' at Loders, close to Netherbury. Isobel Gowdie 'went in to the Downie hills' thus: 'the hill opened, and we came to a fair and large braw room in the day time. There are elf bulls routing and skoyling there at the entry, which feared me.'

Uley Barrow, Gloucestershire **(1869)**

In Tam Lin, the faeries are portrayed as recognisably living beings, rather than ephemeral nature spirits, or aboriginal ghosts; they have their own social structure and ride horses and bear arms as do ordinary mortals; they have the human emotions of love, empathy and anger; their land is not necessarily strange to Tam Lin's experience, being described as 'pleasant'; significantly, while they are able to work their own magic, they do have 'gods' of their own, to whom they must pay a regular tribute. In the Christian era, inevitably, these 'gods' are portrayed as servants of the Devil; their abode is hell.

There is a long tradition of tales of faerie abductions — perhaps the modern equivalent would be the many stories of people who claim to have been abducted by aliens. Child cites some Scandinavian ballads with similar themes and motifs, and makes a good case for Classical antecedents including a Cretan fairy-tale and the pre-Homeric legend of Thetis and Peleus. Walter Scott relates a typical British tale in his *Minstrelsy of the Scottish Border* (1802):

> The wife of a farmer in Lothian had been carried off by the fairies, and, during the year of probation, repeatedly appeared on Sunday, in the midst of her children, combing their hair. On one of these occasions she was accosted by her husband; when she related to him the unfortunate event which had separated them, instructed him by what means he might win her, and exhorted him to exert all his courage, since her temporal and eternal happiness depended on the success of his attempt. The farmer, who ardently loved his wife, set out on Hallowe'en, and, in the midst of a plot of furze, waited impatiently for the procession of the fairies. At the ringing of the fairy bridles, and the wild, unearthly sound which accompanied the cavalcade, his heart failed him, and he suffered the ghostly train to pass by without interruption. When the last had rode past, the whole troop vanished, with loud shouts of laughter and exultation; among which he plainly discovered the voice of his wife, lamenting that he had lost her for ever.

What makes 'Tam Lin' stand out from other tales of elfin abduction, is that the abductee is a male knight who is rescued by his female lover, a reversal of the usual roles (see 'King Orfeo', 'Childe Rowland' and 'Thomas the Rhymer'). Indeed, Janet is one of the strongest female characters in British folklore, feisty both in word and deed. It is perhaps surprising that the verses that express the disdain with which she so forcibly dismisses her family's concerns about her unexpected pregnancy have survived to our modern age, in which such attitudes, if still not socially acceptable in some circles, are frequently not entirely unexpected. Our heroine seeks sexual adventure, finds it, and then is willing to endure a dramatic trial to rescue her lover from a dangerous rival. This fairy-tale, at least, has no need of the revisionist attentions of feminist writers such as Angela Carter!

music page 139

15. Thomas the Rhymer

True Thomas lay on Huntlie bank;
A ferlie he spied wi' his ee;
And there he saw a lady bright,
Come riding down by the Eildon tree.

Her shirt was o' the grass-green silk,
Her mantle o' the velvet yine;
At ilka tett of her horse's mane,
Hung fifty siller bells and nine.

True Thomas, he pulled aff his cap,
And louted low down to his knee,
"All hail, thou mighty Queen of Heaven!
For thy peer on earth I never did see."

"O no, O no, Thomas," she said,
"That name does not belang to me;
I am but the queen of fair Elfland,
That am hither come to visit thee."

"Harp and carp, Thomas," she said,
"Harp and carp along wi' me;
And if ye dare to kiss my lips,
Sure of your body I will be."

Songs from the Magical Tradition

Betide me weal, betide me woe,
That weird shall never daunton me."
Syne he has kissed her rosy lips,
All underneath the Eildon tree.

"Now, ye maun go wi' me," she said;
"True Thomas, ye maun go wi' me;
And ye mann serve me seven years,
Through weal or woe as may chance to be."

She mounted on her milk-white steed;
She's ta'en True Thomas up behind;
And aye, whene'er her bridle rung,
The steed flew swifter than the wind.

O they rade on, and farther on;
The steed gaed swifter than the wind;
Until they reached a desert wide,
And living land was left behind.

"Light down, light down now, True Thomas,
And lean your head upon my knee;
Abide and rest a little space,
And I will shew you ferlies three.

"O see ye not yon narrow road,
So thick beset with thorns and briers?
That is the path of righteousness,
Though after it but few enquires.

And see ye not that braid braid road,
That lies across that lily leven?
That is the path of wickedness,
Though some call it the road to heaven.

And see not ye that bonnie road,
That winds about the ferny brae;
That is the road to fair Elfland,
Where thou and I this night maun gae.

Thomas the Rhymer

But, Thomas, ye maun hold your tongue,
Whatever ye may hear or see;
For, if you speak a word in Elflyn land,
Ye'll ne'er get back to your am countrie."

O they rade on, and farther on,
And they waded through rivers abune the knee,
And they saw neither sun nor moon,
But they heard the roaring of the sea.

It was mirk mirk night, there was nae stern light,
And they waded through red bluid to the knee;
For a' the bluid that's shed on earth
Rins through the springs o' that countrie.

Syne they came to a garden green,
And she pu'd an apple frae a tree—
Take this for thy wages, True Thomas;
It will give thee the tongue that can never lee."

"My tongue is mine am," True Thomas said;
"A gudely gift ye wad gi'e to me!
I neither doughti to buy nor sell,
At fair or tryst where I may be.

I dought neither speak to prince or peer,
Nor ask of grace from fair lady."
"Now hold thy peace!" the lady said,
For as I say, so must it be."

He has gotten a coat of the even cloth,
And a pair of shoes of velvet green;
And till seven years were gane and past,
True Thomas on earth was never seen.

Several different ballad variants of the tale of Thomas the Rhymer exist, the above being taken from Child's collection (#37). Most have broadly the same narrative: they tell how

Songs from the Magical Tradition

Thomas was lying on a grassy bank — in most versions it is Huntly Bank, beneath, or close to, the 'Eildon Tree' — when a lady wearing green silk and silver bells rides by. He bows and hails her as the 'Queen of Heaven', but she explains she is the Queen of Elfland and rather flirtatiously she invites him to kiss her, while warning that he would thence be hers — 'sure of your bodie I will be'. Undeterred, Thomas does as he is bid, and he then has to serve her for seven years. They travel far from mortal realms, and on the way to the land of faerie she shows him a place where the road divides three ways, one of which is narrow, and is the path of righteousness, and another the broad road of wickedness (though some call it heaven); the third road is the path to Elfland. He stays in the faerie realm for seven years, during which time he is forbidden to speak, but when he returns from his sojourn, he wears a livery of grass-green silk, and has the gift of a tongue that cannot lie.

The ballad-poem versions, from which the song is derived, are more varied — one relates that Thomas slept with the queen after which she changed into an ugly hag, but returned to her original beautiful state when they neared her castle, where her husband lived. Thomas stayed at a party in the castle until she told him to return with her, coming back into the mortal realm only to realize that seven years had passed. The journey to Elfland is heavy with symbolism and magical inferences, and involves crossing a barren desert, and rivers running 'with all the blood spilt in anger in the mortal world'. In another version Thomas is said to have returned to Elfland, whence he has not yet returned. It is likely that these ballads were created from earlier tales of encounters with the land of faerie, in order to give a suitably mystical explanation of Thomas' prophetic abilities.

The later ballads actually refer to a real character: Thomas Learmonth of Erceldoune, a medieval Scottish soothsayer. Thomas was born some time in the thirteenth century in Erceldoune, now Earlston in Berwickshire, and had a reputation as the author of many prophetic verses. Little is known for certain of his life but two charters from 1260-80 and 1294 do mention him, the later referring to the 'Thomas de Ercildounson, son and heir of Thome Rymour de Ercildoun'. According to legend he met the Elf Queen who, in return for sexual favours offered to reward him by making him a great harper, or bestowing on him the gift of prophecy. He chose the latter, whereupon he became a sort of Scottish Nostrodamus. It is likely, given Thomas's reputation, that earlier ballads were adapted in order to provide a supernatural explanation for his extraordinary talent.

Rhymers Tower, Earlston, from *Byways of the Scottish Borders* (1886)

His popular acclaim outlived him by several centuries, to the extent that spurious 'prophetic rhymes' have occasionally been fabricated in order to further the cause of Scottish independence. As Chambers notes, 'to fabricate a prophecy in the name of Thomas the Rhymer appears to have been found a good stroke of policy on many occasions'. He became known as 'True Thomas', as in the above version of the song, because was unable to tell a lie. His reputation at one time rivalled that of Merlin, and their prophecies were collected together and published in one volume as early as 1603. He accurately predicted the death of Alexander III (1286), the Battle of Bannockburn (1314), and Scotland's defeat at Flodden (1513). One rather weird connection between Thomas the Rhymer and Merlin is connected with Thomas' prophecy of the union between England and Scotland. He prophesised that the Tweed would meet the Powsail Burn at Drumelzier when England and Scotland had the same king. This was duly achieved in 1603 when the crowns were united, and the Tweed burst its banks in an extraordinary flood and poured into the Powsail Burn at a place known as Merlin's Grave. Another of his prophecies, that one day a bridge would cross the Tweed, and be visible from the Eildon tree, was fulfilled when the Berwickshire Railway Company constructed their graceful 126ft high, nineteen-arch Leaderfoot Viaduct to carry the line between Reston and St Boswells in 1863.

***Rhymer's Glen, Abbotsford,* after Turner**

There is also a specific landscape associated with the legend: the story was given a new lease of life by Sir Walter Scott, who used it in his *Minstrelsy of the Scottish Border* first published in 1804. He named a 'strange secluded ravine' near Abbotsford 'Rhymer's Glen', allegedly because of its associations in local folklore with

Thomas the Rhymer

Thomas. Anthony Roberts, in his *Atlantean Traditions in Ancient Britain* (1975) associates the legend with the Eildon Hills — three large conical hills near Melrose Abbey, which according to the traditional tale recounted by Scott in his *Lay of the Last Minstrel*, were originally one, until the Scottish wizard Michael Scott 'ordered a demon to split them into three'. The site was a hill-fort occupied from the Bronze Age and reused by the Romans, who built a signal tower there. In *Byways of the Scottish Borders* (1886), George Eyre-Todd notes:

> In a grove on the north side of the middle hill the Druids, according to tradition, offered their sacrifices. Underground, too, in the hidden caverns of the mountain, according to the mythic legends which in course of time invested the fate of the hero, King Arthur, and his knights, brought hither by magic means after the last great battle at Camelon, near Falkirk, in which they fell, lie in their armour, waiting for the bugle call that shall break their enchanted sleep and restore them to earthly life once more.
>
> Beside each coal-black courser sleeps a knight,
> A raven plume waves o'er each helmed crest,
> And black the mail which binds each manly breast.
>
> Say, who is he, with summons strong and high,
> That bids the charmed sleep of ages fly,
> Rolls the long sound through Eildon's caverns vast,
> While each dark warrior rouses at the blast,
> His horn, his falcion grasps with mighty hand,
> And peals proud Arthur's march from Fairyland?

The site of the fabled Eildon tree, under which Thomas's meeting with the Elf Queen took place, is marked by the Eildon Tree Stone, a rather disappointing plain grey slab bearing the inscription 'This stone marks the site of the Eildon Tree where legend says Thomas the Rhymer met the Queen of the Fairies and where he was inspired to utter the first notes of the Scottish Muse. Erected by Melrose Literary Society 1929'. It replaced an earlier stone that was noted by J.A. Wade in *A history of Melrose Abbey* in 1861, who described it as 'a large mossy boulder'. There is also Rhymers Tower, the ruins of an old keep on the edge of Earlston village, that was supposedly built by Thomas.

To Robert Graves, the ballad was the very embodiment of his hypothesis that songs in the magical tradition emanate from the witch cult that represented the survival of the Old Religion:

> The Queen of Elfhame was the high priestess of the Scottish witch cult, whose 'gude man', or lover, Thomas became for seven years. Taking a sudden fancy to Thomas, whom she met when out hunting, she introduced him to her secret Court, and announced that he had already taken the necesary oath to her under the elder-tree, this being a tree which symbolised death in the Old Religion. Green was the witches' uniform — hence Robin Hood's Lincoln Green, and the green sleeve of the Maid of Slane. The Queen of Elfhame wore it and made Thomas wear it too. Nine bells hung from her horse's mane because nine was the number sacred to the all-wise Moon-goddess Hecate, with whom Shakespeare identifies the Queen in *Macbeth*.

Journeying into another dimension is not an uncommon theme in British mythology, and was undertaken by several Irish heroes, as well as King Arthur in Welsh legend. It crops up in other ballads of the period such as 'Tam Lin'. It is interesting that the road to 'fair Elfland' is neither the 'road to righteousness' nor the 'road to wickedness', thereby placing the world of faerie outside of orthodox theology as well as physical geography. Parallels may possibly be drawn with the initiatory rites of the mystery religions in the Classical world. Our hero, after a mystical encounter with an otherworldly being, undergoes a dramatic journey through a netherworld, wading through blood, where there is neither sun nor moon, and with the roaring sound of the sea present. Could this be a reference to some drug-induced hallucinatory state that a neophyte was made to undergo as part of some initiatory ritual? Perhaps here the ballads may contain a distant remnant of folk-memory of what it was like to undergo such an ordeal.

music page 140

16. The Two Magicians

The lady stands in her bower door,
As straight as willow wand;
The blacksmith stood a little forebye,
Wi hammer in his hand.

"Weel may ye dress ye, lady fair,
Into your robes o' red;
Before the morn at this same time,
I'll gain your maidenhead."

"Awa, awa, ye coal-black smith,
Woud ye do me the wrang
To think to gain my maidenhead,
That I hae kept sae lang!"

Then she has hadden up her hand,
And she swam by the mold,
"I wudna be a blacksmith's wife
For the full o' a chest o' gold.

I 'd rather I were dead and gone,
And my body laid in grave,
Ere a rusty stock o' coal-black smith
My maidenhead shoud have."

But he has hadden up his hand,
And he sware by the mass,
"I'll cause ye be my light leman
For the hauf o that and less."
O bide, lady, bide,
And aye he bade her bide;
The rusty smith your leman shall be,
For a' your muckle pride.

Then she became a turtle dow,
To fly up in the air,
And he became another dow,
And they flew pair and pair.
O bide, lady, bide ...

She turn'd hersell into an eel,
To swim into yon burn,
And he became a speckled trout,
To gie the eel a turn.
O bide, lady, bide ...

Then she became a duck, a duck,
To puddle in a peel,
And he became a rose-kaimd drake,
To gie the duck a dreel.
O bide, lady, bide ...

She turnd hersell into a hare,
To rin upon yon hill,
And he became a gude grey-hound,
And boldly he did fill.
O bide, lady, bide ...

Then she became a gay grey mare,
And stood in yonder slack,
And he became a gilt saddle,
And sat upon her back.

The Two Magicians

Was she wae, he held her sae,
And still he bade her bide;
The rusty smith her leman was,
For a' her muckle pride.

Then she became a het girdle,
And he became a cake,
And a' the ways she turnd hersell,
The blacksmith was her make.
Was she wae ...

She turnd hersell into a ship,
To sail out ower the flood;
He ea'ed a nail intill her tail,
And syne the ship she stood.
Was she wae ...

Then she became a silken plaid,
And stretchd upon a bed,
And he became a green covering,
And gaind her maidenhead.
Was she wae ...

The song was first published as the 'Twa Magicians' by Peter Buchan in *Ancient Ballads and Songs of the North of Scotland* (1828) and later by Francis Child in *The English and Scottish Popular Ballads*. It may once have been widespread throughout Britain — Cecil Sharp collected a version (also known as 'The Coal Black Smith' from William Sparks, of Minehead, in 1907, and a further Scottish variant was first published in Roy Palmer's *Everyman's Book of British Ballads* in 1980. Child believed it to be an amalgam of two forms of fairy-tale common throughout Europe, which achieved its most graceful ballad form in France. In the first, a couple flee a 'sorcerer, fiend, giant, ogre, rogue', by means of magical transformation; In the second, a young man, apprenticed to a sorcerer, flees from his master, taking refuge by metamorphosis into 'pomegranate kernels, barley-corns, poppy-seeds, millet-grains, pearls; the master becomes a cock, hen, sparrow' and so on, until the pursuer becomes a fox, capable of killing his avian pursuer.

'The Two Magicians' is perhaps one of the few survivors of what Bob Stewart has called the 'magical sequence' song. The narrative in this case parallels the shape-shifting duel between Gwion Bach and Kerridwen which ends in Gwion being consumed by the witch/goddess Kerridwen, who consequently gives birth to Taliesin, greatest of the Welsh bards. Shape-shifting was one of the attributes often attributed to shamans, witches and other practitioners of magic; the ability of a witch to change into a hare to escape attackers is almost ubiquitous in folklore. In most folk tales the transformation is a literal one; in shamanistic terms the soul leaves the unconscious body to enter the body of an animal, fish or bird.

Illustration from Lady Charlotte Guest's *Mabinogion* (1877)

Shape-shifting is part of a mythic story-telling tradition that reaches back over thousands of years. Many gods have this ability, as do heroes of the great epic sagas. In Nordic myth, Odin could change his shape into any beast or bird; the Greek god Zeus often assumed animal shape in his relentless pursuit of young women. In the *Odyssey*, Homer tells of Proteus, a soothsayer who would not give up his knowledge lightly. Menelaus came upon him while he slept, and held on to him tightly as he shape-shifted into various creatures, including a lion, a serpent, a leopard, a pig, and even a tree.

Interestingly the song portrays a contest between two 'secular' magicians, not between a Christian saint and a devil/demon/druid, which one might reasonably expect, it being a scenario common both in folklore and Christian hagiography. The fact that the pursuer is a blacksmith is also of some note. Wayland, or Volund, the metalworking Norse demigod, was himself a captive worker who escaped the evil King Nidud by flying away on birds' wings — a transformation of sorts. What is certain is that the elemental transforming nature of the smith's work adds to the song's magical potency. Could it be that here again we have, in a traditional ballad, echoes of an ancient ritual of magical transformation — perhaps shamanic initiation? Bob Stewart, in *Where is Saint George?* argues that the 'basic images are timeless in that they exist out of historical time or context of religion and cult'. True, but as archetypes in juxtaposition they do provide a perfect framework for a symbolic initiation by trial not just of strength — the stronger pursuing the weaker, — but of intellect: the weaker continually outwits their pursuer with more and more inventive transformations.

There is strong, though inconclusive, archaeological evidence of shamanic practice in the British Bronze Age. In *The Pagan Religions of the Ancient British Isles* (1993) Ronald Hutton describes a round barrow at Upton Lovell in Wiltshire, which contained:

> an adult male skeleton with rows of thin, perforated bones about his neck, thighs and feet. They had almost certainly hung in fringes from his clothes With him were fine stone axe-heads, boars' tusks, white flints and pebbles of a stone not found in the area. A similar mound at Youlgreave, Derbyshire, held a man with the teeth of a dog and a horse under his head and a round bronze amulet on his chest. With him were an ace, quartz pebbles and a piece of porphyry. The ashes of another burial from a lost barrow near Stonehenge were mixed with four stained rectangular bronze tablets, one plain and the others incised with a cross or a star or a lozenge (Bronze Age tarot cards?). All these suggest the presence not so much of a priesthood as of shamans or medicine people, familiar in the tribal peoples of the modern world.

It is possible, even probable, that some vestiges of indigenous pagan practices, including some of its shamanistic aspects, survived down the ages as motifs in folklore, as well as in a few early literary epics such as *Beowulf* and *Taliesin*, and some later ballads which

Songs from the Magical Tradition

Types of barrow — an illustration from Charles Knight's
***Old England, a Pictorial Museum* (1845)**

contain powerful imagery of this kind. Ritual animal disguise was a common expression of folk tradition specifically frowned upon by the Church in the Middle Ages, because of its pagan/shamanistic connotations. It is not too hard to imagine the 'Two Magicians', or at least an ad-lib chant version, forming the 'soundtrack' to some ancient seasonal guising ritual now lost in the mists of time.

This folk-song variant, if such it be, of the Taliesin myth has survived without the ultimate denouement of death and rebirth. Nevertheless the lyrics have a distinctly fatalistic air about them, as if the ending is so pre-determined as to be not worth mentioning. Let us not forget that the act of sexual union — the culmination of the song in the form in which it has survived, has frequently been portrayed as a kind of death in art and literature since time immemorial. The phrase *petit mort* (little death) is still common currency for the timeless moment of orgasm in the French language, as is *la metanza* (the killing) in Spanish. Perhaps, as is sometimes the case when dealing with sex and/or mortality, the unsaid is more eloquent than mere words, and the excising of the final part of the story, in which a form of spiritual re-incarnation may have taken place, has enabled the rest of the ballad to survive relatively unscathed into the Christian era, albeit as a barely understood fragment of pagan oral tradition.

music page 141

17. Widdecombe Fair

"Tom Pearce, Tom Pearce, lend me your grey mare,
All along, down along, out along, lee,
For I want for to go to Widdecombe Fair,
Wi' Bill Brewer, Jan Stewer, Peter Gurney,
Peter Davy, Dan'l Whiddon, Harry Hawke,
Old Uncle Tom Cobley and all,
Old Uncle Tom Cobley and all."

"And when shall I see again my grey mare?"
All along, down along, out along, lee,
"By Friday soon, or Saturday noon,
Wi' Bill Brewer, ...

So they harnessed and bridled the old grey mare
All along, down along, out along, lee,
And off they drove to Widdecombe fair,
Wi' Bill Brewer, ...

Then Friday came, and Saturday noon,
All along, down along, out along, lee,
But Tom Pearce's old mare hath not trotted home,
Wi' Bill Brewer, ...

Songs from the Magical Tradition

So Tom Pearce he got up to the top o' the hill
All along, down along, out along, lee,
And he seed his old mare down a-making her will,
Wi' Bill Brewer, ...

And how did he know it was his grey mare?
All along, down along, out along, lee,
"Cos one foot was shod and the other was bare.
Wi' Bill Brewer, ...

So Tom Pearce's old mare, her took sick and died,
All along, down along, out along, lee,
And Tom he sat down on a stone, and he cried
Wi' Bill Brewer, ...

But this isn't the end o' this shocking affair,
All along, down along, out along, lee,
Nor, though they be dead, of the horrid career
Wi' Bill Brewer, ...

When the wind whistles cold on the moor of the night,
All along, down along, out along, lee,
Tom Pearce's old mare doth appear gashly white,
Wi' Bill Brewer, ...

And all the long night he heard skirling and groans,
All along, down along, out along, lee,
From Tom Pearce's old mare in her rattling bones,
Wi' Bill Brewer, ...

The tale of Tom Cobley, and his mysterious disappearance along with his companions, and the borrowed grey mare, is certainly Devon's most famous song. Although it is believed to be much earlier, it was not published until the late nineteenth century — in 1880 by Mr W. Davies. It was the Revd Sabine Baring-Gould's book *Songs of the West*, first published in 1890, that brought it to a wider audience. Baring-Gould collected it in 1888 from one W. F. Collier of Woodtown on Dartmoor, though

Widdecombe Fair

he acknowledged that different versions existed in other places, including Cornwall, Somerset, Bedfordshire and Sussex. Included in the various casts in these versions were such notables as Uncle Tom Cobbler and Uncle Tom Cockerell. In the Cotswold version, 'Stow Fair', 'Cobley' becomes 'Uncle Tom Goblin'. The song also appears in Cecil Sharp's *Folk Songs from Somerset* (1905).

The story is simple enough — Tom Cobley and his friends ask Tom Pearce if they can borrow his grey mare to get to the fair. They agree that the horse will be returned by midday on Saturday. When the horse and its companions fail to return, Tom Pearce sets out to find them. On reaching the top of Widecombe Hill he sees the horse 'making its will' after which it falls sick and dies. The song concludes with the ghost of Tom's old mare which is said to appear 'when the wind whistles cold on the moor at night', and 'in her rattling bones'. Presumably, the horse would have been used to pull a gig, as seven men would not have all been able to ride the mare at once, as is depicted on the humorous image that appears all around the village, including on the village sign.

Many people have researched the history of the song, and it does appear that the characters in the song lyrics were actually based on real people from mid and north Devon. Most have names which can be traced to families living or working in the northern fringes of Dartmoor in the early 1800s, and both a Bill Brewer and a Tom Pearce lived in Sticklepath, where the Pearce family owned a mill at which the mare was supposed to have been stabled. There is a sign at the Tom Cobley Tavern at Spreyton, which records that all the characters left from outside that pub in 1802 to go to Widecombe (note the current spelling of the village's name differs from that in the song title). This is probably the earliest date referenced with regard to the song, though its provenance is, of course, somewhat dubious. The name Thomas Cobley (or Cobleigh) was then quite common in the Spreyton area, and there is the grave of one of them who died in 1844, at the age of eighty-two years, apparently having inherited his great uncle's estate at Butsford. There are also many graves of Davys, Gurneys, Pearces and Stewers in mid-Devon churchyards, whose descendents still exist in the area. It was the great uncle from Butsford, however, who is supposed to have been the Tom Cobley of the song. He, apparently died at Spreyton in 1794, but the whereabouts of his grave is unknown.

Two typical postcards from the early 20th century, one claiming to show the man himself, the other the Cobley family grave at Spreyton.

For many years people from mid and north Devon travelled to the annual livestock sale at Widecombe at the end of every summer to trade their goods for sheep. This cross-country journey forms the basis of the story in the song. There were many autumn fairs all over Dartmoor at which farmers would sell surplus stock, with Widecombe being perhaps the best known. Widecombe and Spreyton were only about twelve miles from each other across the moor — a reasonable distance to drive a flock of sheep or a herd of cattle. However, it was not until Saturday 19 October 1850 that the *Exeter and Plymouth Gazette* first announced that a 'Free Fair' would be held on the green at Widecombe. The following Saturday the same paper reported 'A cattle fair was held at Widecombe-in-the-Moor for the first time on Tuesday last'. It was said to have been a busy affair with a large attendance of yeomen and gentlemen of the district where 736 sheep, 1,507 cattle, and fifty ponies were put under the hammer. The paper noted that due to its success the fair should be 'permanently established'. This dating rather throws a spanner in the works regarding the aforementioned characters from Spreyton and Sticklepath. Perhaps the song originally referred to a fair in a different location that eventually became overshadowed by the one at Widecombe. Tavistock's annual Goosey Fair, which dates back to the twelfth century might possibly be a candidate, but unless some alternative lyrics of earlier provenance turn up this can, of course, only be speculation. The folk song 'Tavistock Goosey Fair' was written by C. John Trythall and first published in 1912.

Whether there actually was a real incident on which the song is based is also debatable. Certainly the story is plausible enough, given the many tales of smuggling, murder and banditry told about Dartmoor in the eighteenth and nineteenth centuries. Perhaps the mare was stolen, or lost, and the men were too ashamed to return and tell the owner. Perhaps they imbibed rather too much of the Devonshire cider and lost their way on the moor, falling prey to one of its infamous mires, as described by Conan-Doyle in his classic tale *The Hound of the Baskervilles* (1902). However, if the song was based on a real incident, and men had gone missing, one would have expected it to have appeared in a broadsheet or newspaper of the day, and nobody has yet discovered such a document. Could it be, perhaps, that the song's origins have a more ancient and archetypal origin?

There is a theory, related by Paul Devereux in his book *Spirit Roads*, that could place the song's origins much further back in time, and across to the continent of Europe. In the book he discusses a paper by noted folklorist Theo Brown who writes that the concept of a spectral grey/white horse came from mainland Europe. It is suggested that the principal motif of the song came to Dartmoor

Songs from the Magical Tradition

with German immigrants who worked in Dartmoor's tin and copper mines in the Elizabethan period. Some were miners from the Harz mountains where (along with many other European regions) there existed a tradition of *der Schimmelreiter*, a ghostly grey horse and rider which would lead the souls of the departed to the realms of the dead. As the core concept of the belief was that the grey mare represented an entity that hovered between life and death and acted as a 'boundary figure', a guide without which no human soul could be led into the afterlife, in the context of the song Tom Pearce may have 'sat down on a stone' and 'cried', because he realized that the grey mare's death meant the spirits of Tom Cobley and his friends, who presumably had died mysteriously on the moor, would have no such guide. It may even be that his grief was extended to all the future spirits of the dead who from now on would wander, guideless in oblivion. In Britain, the *Mari Lwyd* (Grey Mare) ceremonies in Wales, and the Hooden Horse tradition of south-east England may preserve feint echoes of such beliefs.

Spirit ways, or corpse roads — processional routes along which the dead were taken to their final resting place, were possibly the original purpose of the ancient stone rows that litter the Dartmoor landscape, many of which are associated with barrow graves. They were certainly an important part of funerary rites in the Viking tradition, and elements of such practices survived of necessity in remote areas long enough to enter the Christian tradition as 'church-way paths'. Shakespeare's lines from *A Midsummer Night's Dream* (c. 1595), spoken by Puck, leave little room for doubt that such physical routes were still regarded as spirit paths according to the folklore of his day:

> Now it is the time of night,
> That the graves all gaping wide,
> Every one lets forth his sprite,
> In the church-way paths to glide.

Interestingly, one such route is known to exist close to Widecombe; it is mentioned in Robert Dymond's *Things New and Old Concerning the Parish of Widecombe-in-the-Moor* (1876):

Widdecombe Fair

About half way up the steep ascent from Dartmeet, the road seeks an easier gradient by a bend towards the left. Pedestrians, however, commonly take the straighter but steeper course on the turf. Close by the track which cuts off the bend in the road are two large masses of granite, which were evidently united in one block at some remote time. The larger of these measures 8½ feet by 3. The other is triangular in form, about 6 by 3½ feet. Their upper surfaces will be found studded with rudely cut crosses and letters. The corpses of parishioners who died in the large district beyond the East and West Dart, formerly attached to Widecombe, had to be carried by hand a long and toilsome journey to the parish church. On this stone the bearers laid the coffin,— the Dart sparkling below and the solemn moor all round,— while they beguiled their rest by chiselling the initial letters of their dead friend's name.

The Widecombe 'Coffin Stone'

Before 1260, all burials within the Forest of Dartmoor took place at the parish church of Lydford, The route to which, as used by those who lived on the eastern side of the moor, was named, as is traditional, the 'Lych Way'; it originated near Bellever and would have normally crossed the rivers West Dart, Cowsic, Walkham

Songs from the Magical Tradition

and Tavy. However, heavy rain would frequently add up to six miles to the journey, in order that suitable crossing places on the swollen rivers could be found. In 1260, Bishop Bronescombe of Exeter gave permission for those living in the hamlets of Babeny and Pizwell to be buried at Widecombe, thus avoiding the arduous journey across the moor to Lydford. This was soon afterwards extended to all parishes on the eastern side of Dartmoor.

Could the Coffin Stone be the one upon which Tom Cobley sat down and cried? It does seem at least plausible that a very ancient concept may underpin this darkly humorous tale of missing travellers and a ghostly Dartmoor horse. Or, it could conceivably be an example of a song creating its own folklore rather than, more usually, the other way round. While there are plenty of folk tales told about Widecombe and its surrounding moors, ghostly equine apparitions do not tend to figure among them.

Much Widecombe folklore stems from a fierce storm that hit the town in 1638, killing four, and injuring 62 inhabitants, most of whom were attending Sunday service. The tower was struck by lightning and part of it crashed through the roof. Reports tell of a strange darkness, powerful thunder, and a 'great ball of fire' that ripped through the church. Predictably, perhaps, the Devil was held responsible: having come to claim an errant parishioner as his own, he made a hasty departure, forgetting that he had tethered his horse to a stone pinnacle on the tower.

The Devon Regiment of Volunteers supposedly marched to the tune of 'Widdecombe Fair' in 1899 during the Boer War, while Exeter City football club used to play the song before every match, until they hit a losing streak and thought the song may have had something to do with their misfortune! The story is supposed to have inspired Alfred Hitchcock's *The Farmer's Wife*, as well as Eden Philpot's novel *Widecombe Fair*. More recently Steve Knightley of the duo Show of Hands wrote a very spooky song based on the tale, full of darkness and menace, imagining what might have happened out on the moor, on the way to the fair.

The Music

The Abbot's Bromley Horn Dance	142
The Astrologer	128
The Bells of Paradise	128
The Boar's Head Carol	129
Childe Rowland	129
Clerk Colvill	132
The Cutty Wren	132
The Faery Dance	143
Hal-An-Tow	133
Harvest Home (hornpipe)	143
Harvest Home (polka)	146
The Helston Furry Dance	146
Jennifer Gentle	134
John Barleycorn	135
The King of the Faeries	144
King Orfeo	136
Lady Margaret	136
The Lambton Worm	137
Sheebeg Sheemore	145
Sir John Barleycorn	134
Somerset Wassail	138
Tam Lin	139
Tam Lin (reel)	142
Thomas rhe Rhymer	139
The Two Magicians	140
Widdecombe Fair	141

Songs from the Magical Tradition

1. The Astrologer

It's of a bold ast-ro-lo-ger in Lon-don town did dwell. At tell-ing maid-ens' for-tunes, there's none could him ex-cel, There was a nice young serv-ing girl a-liv-ing there close by, She came one day to the ast-rol-og-er all for to have a try.

2. The Bells of Paradise

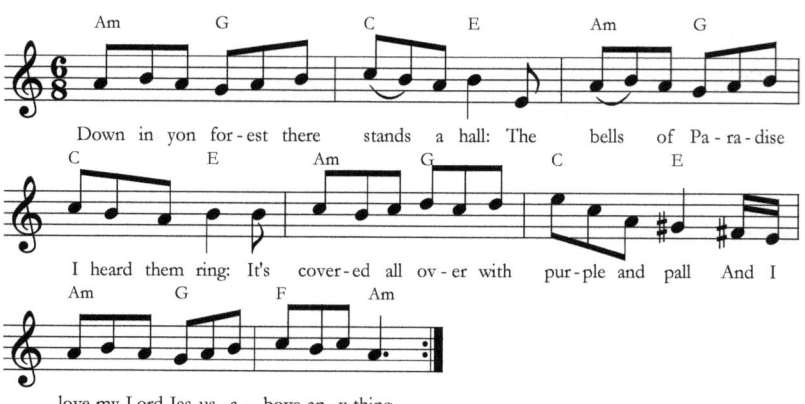

Down in yon for-est there stands a hall: The bells of Pa-ra-dise I heard them ring: It's cover-ed all ov-er with pur-ple and pall And I love my Lord Jes-us a-bove an-y-thing.

The Music

3. The Boar's Head Carol

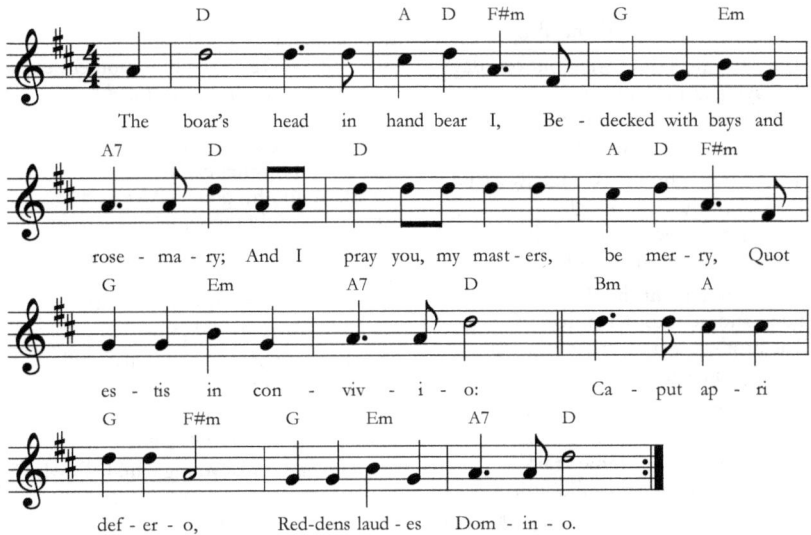

4. Childe Rowland

Words and music transcribed from Maria Cunningham's reconstructed version on her album *Albion's Words* (2011).

Songs from the Magical Tradition

Three brothers lived in Bonny Carlisle
Of noble blood and true
Likewise their sister Burd Ellen
The Fairest amongst them all

These brothers three went out one day
A-playing at the ball
Fair Ellen joined them in their sport
Beside the high church wall

The youngest brother Childe Rowland
He kicked the ball so high
Right up and over the high church spire
Childe Rowland made it fly.

Round and about the church they went
Ellen and her brothers three
The brothers san by way of the sun
But a-widdershins Ellen ran she.

These brothers three they found their ball
Beside the white church gate
But Ellen she ne'er came again
Though long time they did wait

They sought her east, they sought her west
They sought her up and down
Woe were the hearts of these brothers true,
For she was not to be found.

Unto the wise sage Merlin
The oldest brother came
To ask of him his good advice
Why his sister's not come home.

"A-widdershins fair Ellen ran
About the churchyard wall,
Now the king of Elfin-land
Has her imprisoned in his hall"

"What can be done", said the eldest son
"to free my sister dear?
Oh tell me what I have to do
And nothing will I fear."

The wise sage Merlin shook his head
"Two things you must first learn,
If you would go into Elfin-land
And come safely home again."

And when this brother had well learned
These things he had to do.
He's bid farewell to his mother dear,
On his journey he did go.

They waited long, and longer still
In doubt and grief and pain,
But woe was the heart of his mother dear,
For he came not home again.

Unto the wise sage Merlin
The second brother came
To ask of him his good advice
And he was told the same.

And when this brother had well learned
These things he had to do.
He's followed after his brother dear,
On his journey he did go.

But they waited long and longer still,
His mother and his brother young,
But woe was within their hearts,
For he came not home again.

Then up and spoke young Childe Rowland
He was the youngest son,
"I will go into Elfin-land
And bring my siblings home."

His mother sighed a weary sigh,
The thought it gave her pain,
But she gave to him his father's sword
That never struck in vain.

And unto the wise sage Merlin
This youngest brother came
To ask of him his good advice
For to bring his siblings home.

And Merlin said "There are two things
That you must understand,
If you would go into Elfinland
And come safely home again.

Bite no bite nor drink no drink
As you go along your way,
And everyone to whom you speak
With your good sword you must slay."

Childe Rowland mounted on his horse
With his father's sword in hand
And with words of thanks upon his lips
He rode off to Elfin-land.

From north to south and round about

The Music

Then roved this youngest son.
And after many weary miles
Into Elfin-land he came.

And the first one that he met and asked
Was tending his horses fine.
Says "I know not of the king's dark tower
Ask the lad that tends the swine."

Then he took out his father's sword
That never struck in vain
And there cut off the horse-herd's head
And left him dead and slain.

And everyone that he did meet
Along his weary way,
He's asked of them this same question,
And with his good sword he did slay.

The last he asked was a woman wise,
Her hands about her feet
She gave to him some sage advice,
When Childe Rowland she did meet.

"A little further on you'll find
A hill so round and green,
From top to bottom ringed around,
The finest to be seen.

Circle three times round about
A-widdershins you must go,
Crying, Open Door, Open Door, Let me in!
And then it shall be so."

Childe Rowland took his father's sword
That never struck in vain,
And he's cut off the hen-wife's head
And he's left her dead and slain.

Soon he's come to the round, round hill,
Its sides so soft and green,
And he a-circled agains the sun,
Crying "Open and let me in!"

And then a great door opened
In the hill's green grassy side,
And into the depths came Childe Rowland
His siblings there to find.

The walls were lined with stone so fine
That shone like diamonds bright
And rosy glowed the fine warm air
Like the sunset before night.

Then into the elf-king's hall
This youngest son did go

And here before saw his sister dear
Sitting on a couch of gold.
She said "Pity you poor luckless fool
Why stayed you not at home?
For come the king of Elf-land in
Your fortune is forlorn."

Childe Rowland told his sister fair
Of his journey long and hard
"Oh how I hunger, Ellen dear,
Come bring to me some food."

Poor Ellen heard the words he spoke
And they gave to her much pain,
But under the spell of Elfin-land
To warn him was in vain.

But when she brought to him the bowl
Sage Merlin he did see,
"No food nor drink will I here eat,
Till my siblings I set free."

Then its "Fee Fie Fo Fum
I smell the blood of Childe Rowland"
[spoken]

And in then came the elfin king
With his mighty sword so fine.
"Bow down to me young Childe Rowland
For your blood it shall be mine!"

Childe Rowland's took his father's sword
And he's held it up on high
"Oh king" he says, "I fear thee not
And I surely shall not die.

Wake my brothers from their sleep,
Free my sister from your spell,
For we would go from out this land
Back through the gates of Hell."

Then up and spoke the Elfin king
"You've learned your lessons well,
And for your courage I have seen
I'll release them from my spell."

The king raised up his arms on high
And he's uttered words of power.
They found themselves on the hillside green
All at the noon-tide hour.

Northwards these three brothers went
In the light of the summer sun
Along with them Burd Ellen went
As from Elfland she was won.

Songs from the Magical Tradition

5. Clerk Colvill

6. The Cutty Wren

The Music

7. Hal-An-Tow

Take no scorn to wear the horn
That was the crest when you were born,
Your father's father wore it
And your father wore it too.
Chorus
Robin Hood and Little John
Have both gone to the Fair O,
And we will to the merry green wood
To hunt the buck and hare O
Chorus

And where are all the Spaniards
That made so great a boast, O?
They shall eat the feathered goose
And we shall eat the roast, O
Chorus
God bless Aunt Mary Moses
And all her power and might, O,
And send us peace in Merry England
Send peace by day and night, O.
Chorus

Songs from the Magical Tradition

8. Jennifer Gentle

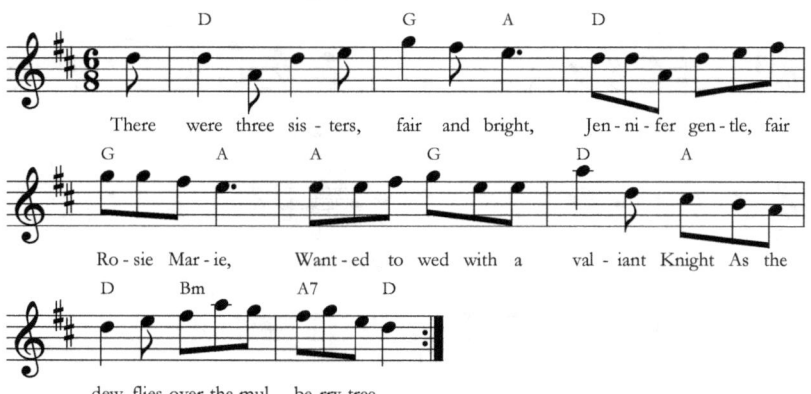

9a. Sir John Barleycorn

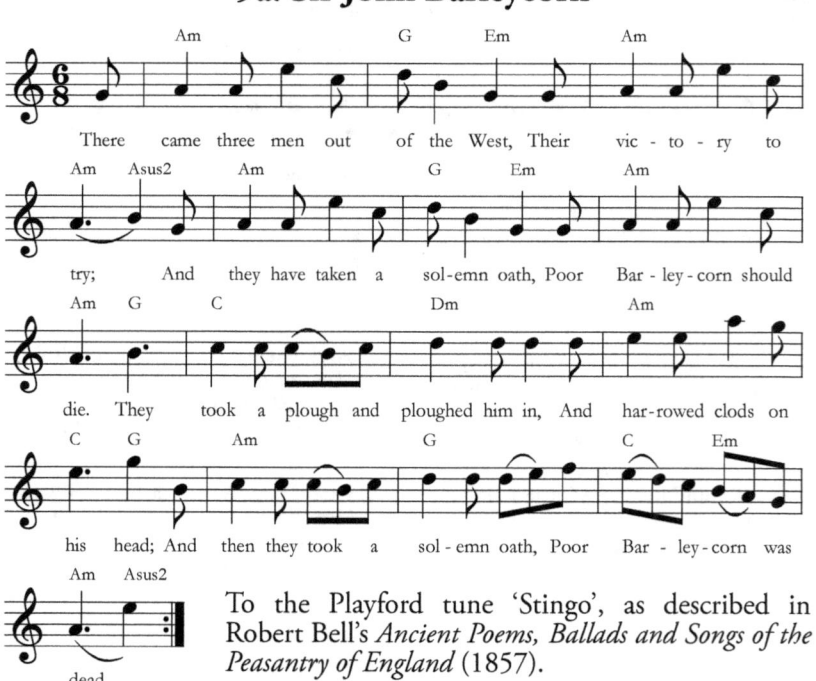

To the Playford tune 'Stingo', as described in Robert Bell's *Ancient Poems, Ballads and Songs of the Peasantry of England* (1857).

9b. John Barleycorn

They've let him lie for a very long time,
'Til the rain from heaven did fall
And little sir john sprung up his head
And so amazed them all
They let him stand 'til midsummer's day
'Til he looked both pale and wan
And little sir john grew a long long beard
And so become a man

They hired men with their scythes so sharp
To cut him off at the knee
They rolled him and tied him by the waist,
And served him barbarously
They hired men with sharp pitchforks
Who pricked him to the heart
But the loader he served him worse than that
For he bound him to a cart

They wheeled him around and around a field
'Til they came unto a barn
And there they made a solemn oath
On poor John Barleycorn
They hired men with their crabtree sticks
To cut him skin from bone
But the miller he served him worse than that
For he ground him between two stones

Here's little Sir John and the nut brown bowl,
Here's brandy in the glass
For little Sir John and the nut brown bowl
Proved the strongest man at last
For the huntsman he can't hunt the fox
Nor loudly blow his horn
And the tinker he can't mend kettles or pots
Without a little Barleycorn

Songs from the Magical Tradition

10. King Orfeo

11. Lady Margaret

Words and tune transcribed from James Findlay's album *As I Carelessly Did Stray* (2010).

The Music

12. The Lambton Worm

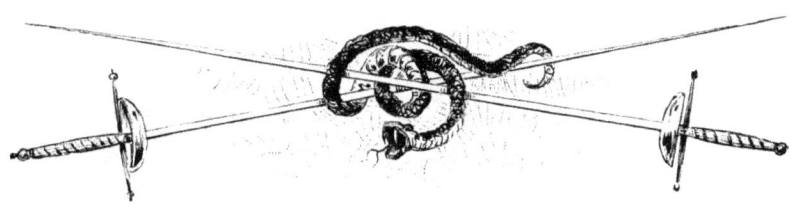

Songs from the Magical Tradition

13. The Somerset Wassail

Wass-ail and Wass-ail all o-ver the town! The cup it is white and the ale it is brown; The cup it is made of the good ash-en tree, And so is the malt of the best bar-ley: For it's your wass-ail, and it's our wass-ail! And it's joy be to you, and jol-ly wass-ail!

14. Tam Lin

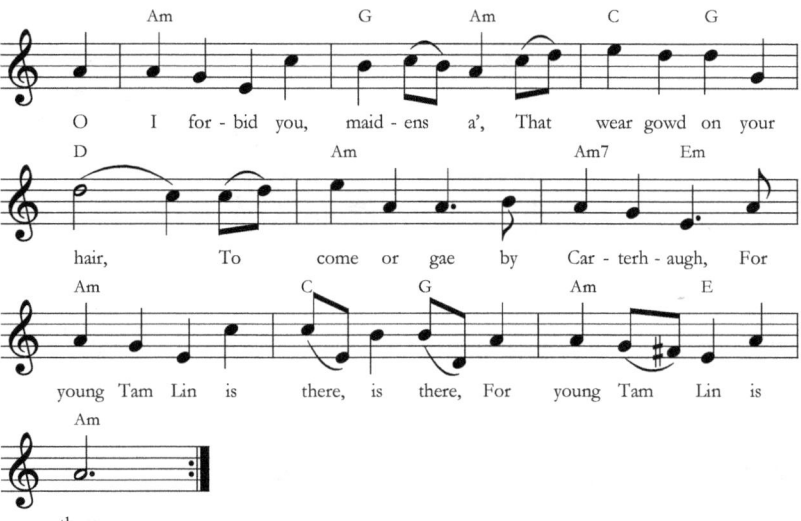

Tune transcribed from James Findlay's album *Sport and Play* (Fellside, 2011). Note how the last line of each verse is repeated.

15. Thomas the Rhymer

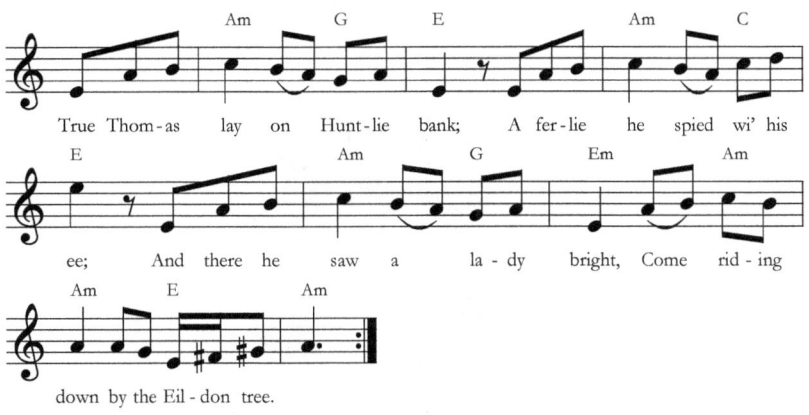

Songs from the Magical Tradition

16. The Two Magicians

The sixth verse is printed here. The first five verses are generally sung without the 'Bide, Lady, Bide' refrain.

17. Widdecombe Fair

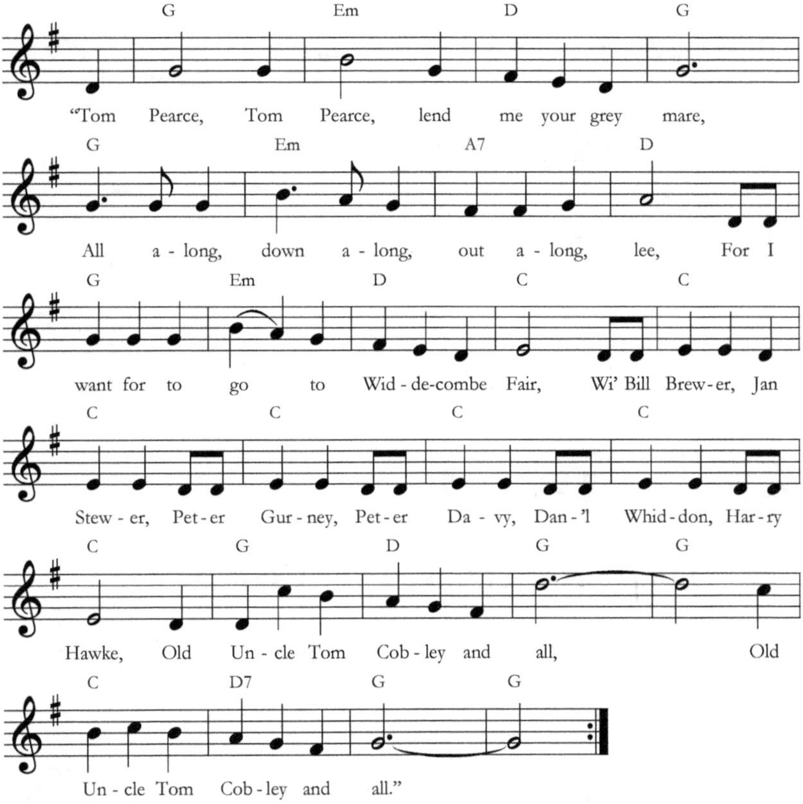
G Em D G
"Tom Pearce, Tom Pearce, lend me your grey mare,
G Em A7 D
All a - long, down a - long, out a - long, lee, For I
G Em D C C
want for to go to Wid - de-combe Fair, Wi' Bill Brew-er, Jan
C C C C
Stew - er, Pet - er Gur - ney, Pet - er Da - vy, Dan - 'l Whid - don, Har - ry
C G D G G
Hawke, Old Un - cle Tom Cob - ley and all, Old
C D7 G G
Un - cle Tom Cob - ley and all."

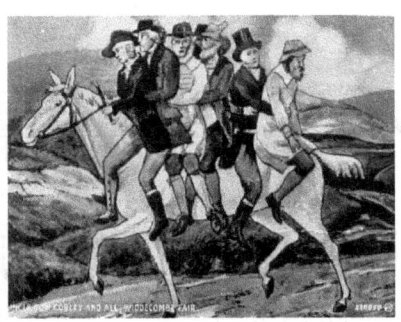

Songs from the Magical Tradition

The Abbots Bromley Horn Dance

See page 50.

Tam Lin's Reel (a.k.a. The Glasgow Reel)

See page 101.

Played fast, in D minor, then transposed to A minor and back again.

Harvest Home (hornpipe)

See page 61. Play fast, with a 'dotted' hornpipe rhythm.

The Faery Dance (a.k.a. Old Molly Hare)

Pg. 67.

Songs from the Magical Tradition

The King of the Faeries

A lovely old tune — play it either as a slow air, or fast, with a 'dotted' rhythm, as a hornpipe. Note the key change in the 'B' music.

Sheebeg Sheemore (Si Bheag Si Mhor)

Reputedly the first piece ever written by Turlough Carolan (1670-1738). A magnificent, stately air. The title means 'The big and the small faery hills' (see page 67). No wonder people thought his talent was given to him by the faeries — not many musicians can claim an internationally loved masterpiece as their first composition!

Songs from the Magical Tradition

Harvest Home (polka)

See page 61. A rollicking polka from Dorset.

The Helston Furry Dance

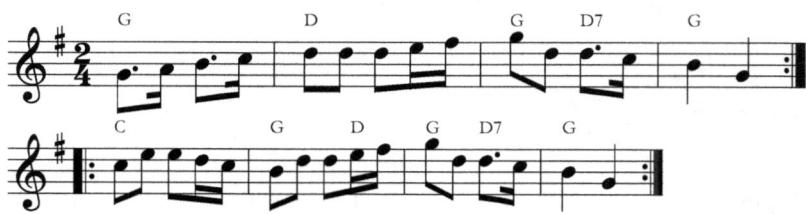

The traditional tune for the processional dance (see pages 44-7).

Bibliography

Aburrow, Yvonne. *Auguries & Omens*, Capall Bann (1994)
Alexander, Marc. *Folklore, Myths & Customs of Britain*, Sutton (2002)
Anon.. *Legend Land* Vol. 2, Great Western Railway (1922)
ASH Consulting Group, 'The Borders Landscape Assessment' *Scottish Natural Heritage Review*, No.112 (1998)
Baker, Margaret. *Discovering the Folklore & Customs of Love and Marriage*, Shire (1974)
Baring-Gould, Sabine. *Folk Songs of the West Country*, David & Charles (1974)
Bell, Robert (ed.). *Ancient Poems Ballads and Songs of the Peasantry of England*, Parker (1857)
Bird, Jerry. *Landscape of Memory*, Green Magic (2009)
——. 'The Devil & St Pancras', *Merry Meet Magazine* 47 (2012)
Child, Francis James (ed.). *The English & Scottish Popular ballads*, Folklore Press/Pageant Book Company (1957)
——. *The English & Scottish Popular ballads*, Vol. 2 Loomis House (2002)
Dames, Michael. *Taliesin's Travels*, Heart of Albion Press (2006)
Davies, Owen. *Grimoires – a History of Magic Books*, OUP (2009)
——. *Popular Magic – Cunning Folk in English History*, Hambledon (2007)
Day, Kenneth F. Eden *Phillpotts on Dartmoor*, David & Charles (1981)
Deane, Tony and Shaw, Tony. *The Folklore of Cornwall*, Batsford (1975)
Dearmer, P. Vaughan Williams, R. and Shaw, M. *The Oxford Book of Carols*, OUP (1935)
Devereux, Paul. The Secret History of Corpse Ways *3rd Stone*, 41 6-10 (2001)
——. *Spirit Roads*, Collins & Brown (2007)
Dymond, R. (ed.) *Things New and Old Concerning the Parish of Widecombe-in-the-Moor and its Neighbourhood*, Torquay Directory Company (1876)
Eyre-Todd, George. *Byways of the Scottish Border*, Selkirk (1886)
Frazer, James. *The Golden Bough*, MacMillan (1941)
Freeman, Richard. *Explore Dragons*, Heart of Albion Press (2006)
Froome, Joyce. *Songs of Witchcraft and Magic*, Museum of Witchcraft (2007)
Gilchrist, Annie. pp 52-56 J*ournal of the Folk-Song Society*, No. 14 (1910)
Glosecki, S.O. *Shamanism and Old English Poetry*, Garland (1989)
Gosse, Philip Henry. *Sea and Land*, James Nisbet (1864)
Graves, Robert. *English & Scottish Ballads* Heinemann (1982)
——. *The White Goddess*, Faber (1948)
Grose, Francis. *The Antiquities of England & Wales*, Kessinger (2008)
Hardy, Thomas. *Tess of the D'Urbervilles*, Macmillan (1902)
Harris, J. *The Ballad and Oral Literature*, Harvard (1991)
Harte, Jeremy. *Cuckoo Pounds & Singing Barrows*, DNH&AS (1986)
——. *Explore Fairy Traditions*, Heart of Albion Press (2004)
Herbert, Kathleen. *Looking for the Lost Gods of England*, Anglo-Saxon Books (1994)
Hicks, Peter. *Uncle Tom Cobley: Widecombe in the Moor* (1996)
Hole, Christina. *A Dictionary of Folk Customs*, Helicon (1976)
Hunt, Robert. *Popular Romances of the West of England*, Chatto & Windus (1930)
Hutton, Ronald. *Stations of the Sun*, OUP (1996)
——. *The Pagan Religions of the Ancient British Isles*, Blackwell (1991)
——. *The Triumph of the Moon*, OUP (1997)
Jacobs, Joseph. *English Folk and Fairy Tales* Abela (2009)
Jennings, Pete. *Old Glory & The Cutty Wren* Gruff (2003)

Knowles, Elizabeth. *Oxford Dictionary of Phrase and Fable*, OUP (2005)
Lloyd, A.L. *Folk Song in England*, Lawrence & Wishart (1967)
MacKillop, James. *Dictionary of Celtic Mythology* Oxford (1998)
Maltwood, Katherine. *Enchantments of England* James Clarke (1982)
Morrish, John (ed.). *The Folk Handbook*, Backbeat Books (2007)
Murray, Margaret. *The God of the Witches*, Faber & Faber (1956)
O'Connor, Mike *Ilow Kernow 3*, Lyngham House (2005)
Opie, Peter & Iona. *The Oxford Book of Nursery Rhymes*, Oxford (1951)
Palmer, Roy. *Everyman's Book of British Ballads*, Dent (1980)
Pennick, Nigel. *Crossing the Borderlines*, Capall Bann (1998)
Pegg, Bobb. *Rites and Riots*, Blandford (1981)
Percy, Thomas. *Reliques of Ancient English Poetry*, Routledge (1857)
Playford, John *Playford's Dancing Master*, Faber (2007)
Porter, John. *Anglo-Saxon Riddles*, Anglo-Saxon Books (1995)
Quiller-Couch, Arthur. *The Oxford Book of Ballads*, Oxford Clarendon Press (1910)
Rickert, Edith. *Ancient English Christmas Carols 1400-1700*, Chatto & Windus (1910)
Roberts, Anthony. *Atlantean Traditions in Ancient Britain*, Rider (1975)
Robbins, Rossell Hope. *Secular Lyrics of the XIVth and XVth Centuries*, Clarendon Press (1952)
Scott, Walter. *Letters on Demonology and Witchcraft*, Ace (1970)
——. *Minstrelsey of the Scottish Border*, Murray (1869)
Sharp, Cecil. *Folk Songs From Somerset*, Simpkin (1910)
Simpson, Jaqueline & Roud, Steve. *Oxford Dictionary of English Folklore*, OUP (2000)
St Leger-Gordon, Ruth. *The Witchcraft and Folklore of Dartmoor*, Alan Sutton (1982)
Stewart, Bob. *Where is Saint George?* Moonraker Press (1977)
Thiselton Dyer, R.F. *Folk-lore of Shakespeare*, Griffith & Farran (1883)
Trubshaw, Bob. *Explore Folklore*, Heart of Albion Press (2003)
——. 'Hollow Hills', *At The Edge*, 5 (1997)
Vaughan Williams, R. & Lloyd, A.L. *The Penguin Book of English Folk Songs* Penguin (1990)
Wade, James. *A History of Melrose Abbey*, Jack (1861)
Westwood, Jennifer. *Albion*, Granada (1985)
Westwood, Jennifer & Simpson, Jaqueline. *The Lore of the Land*, Penguin (2005)
Whistler, Laurence. *The English Festivals* Heinemann (1942)
Whitlock, Ralph. *The Folklore of Devon*, Batsford (1977)
Wilby, Emma. *Cunning Folk and Familiar Spirits: Shamanistic Visionary Traditions in Early Modern British Witchcraft and Magic*, Sussex Academic Press (2005)
Wood, Peter. 'John Barleycorn: The Evolution of a Folk-song Family' *Folk Music Journal* 8/4 (2004)

Websites Consulted:

www.bl.uk
www.bodley.ox.ac.uk/ballads
www.contemplator.com/carolan
www.EFDSS.org
www.folklore-society.com
www.folkmusic.net
www.fromoldbooks.com
www.gippeswic.demon.co.uk
www.gutenberg.com
www.historic-uk.com/CultureUK
www.humanities.mcmaster.ca
www.hymnsandcarolsofchristmas.com
www.legendarydartmoor.co.uk
www.mudcat.org
www.mysteriousbritain.co.uk/scotland
www.nls.uk/auchinleck
www.oldmusicproject.com
www.sacred-texts.com
www.tam-lin.org
www.thesession.org
www.traditionalmusic.co.uk
www.widecombe-in-the-moor.com

Index

Abbots Bromley Horn Dance, 50, 142
Adderbury, 38
Apple orchards, 84-93
Arthur, 27, 29, 68, 92, 111, 112
The Astrologer, 1-6, 128
Baring-Gould, Sabine, 46, 48, 58-9, 120
Barrett, Francis, 3
Barrows, 29, 67, 103, 117, 124
Bell, Robert, 47-8, 59
The Bells of Paradise, 7-10, 128
Beltane (see May Day)
Beowulf, 18, 84, 117
Blood, 10, 25-6, 69, 108, 112
The Boar's Head Carol, 11-20 , 129
Broadwood, Lucy, 55
Burial Mounds (see barrows)
Burns, Robert, 59, 100
Carolan, Turlough, 67, 145
Carthy, Martin, 27
Cauldrons, 18, 38, 41
Celtic Mythology, 10, 41, 65, 68
Celtic Paganism, 62, 70
Celtic races, 19, 93
Child, Francis, 26-7, 32, 34, 53-6, 64, 67, 69, 73-5, 79, 100-3, 107, 115
Childe Rowland, 21-30, 104, 129
Christian Church, 2, 10, 29, 42, 46, 50, 67, 70, 86, 118
Christmas, 9, 10, 13-15, 19, 41, 53, 85-6
Church-way paths (see corpse roads)
Clerk Colin (see *Clerk Colvill*)
Clerk Colvin (see *Clerk Colvill*)
Clerk Colvill, 31-7, 132
Cornwall, 32, 35, 43-50, 92, 121
Corpse Roads, 124-6
Corpus Christi , 8- 9
Cunningham, Maria, 30, 129, 139
Crying the Neck, 60-61
The Cutty Wren, 37-42, 132
Dance, 42, 44-8, 50, 61, 67, 85
Dartmoor, (see Widdecombe Fair)
Davies, Gilbert, 48, 53, 55
Davies, Owen, 6
Dearmer, Percy, 12
Devil, the, 14, 30, 41, 49, 79, 103, 116, 126
The Devil's Nine Questions, 54
Down in Yon Forest (see *Bells of Paradise*)
Druids, 23, 27, 94, 111, 116
Duncan, Helen, 4
Dymond, Robert, 124
Easter, 9
Elfhame, 112
The Elfin Knight, 54, 56
Eucharist, 8-9
Faeries, 27-9, 63-6, 100-3, 108, 112
The Faery Dance, 63, 67, 143
Findlay, James, 73, 93, 136, 139
Fisher King, 10
Folk ritual, 30, 39-42, 44-7, 70, 81, 84, 86-9, 92, 118
Frazer, Sir James, 40, 42, 61-2
Froome, Joyce, 6
Furry Dance, 44-8, 146
Gardiner, George, 1
Ghosts, 69, 71-6, 92, 103-4, 121, 124
Giles Collins, 10, 33
Gimmel Rings, 75-6
The Glasgow Reel (see *Tam Lin*)
Goddesses, 10, 41, 44, 112, 116
Graves, Robert, 34, 112
Hal an Tow, 43-50, 133
Hammond, Henry, 1
Hardy, Thomas, 5
Harps, 63-4, 66-8, 70, 109
Harvest Home (tunes), 143, 146
Harvest Home celebrations, 61

149

Harvesting, 49, 60-62, 90, 94,
Helston, (see *Hal an Tow/ Furry Dance*)
Hill-forts, 29, 81, 111
Hollow Hills, 29
Holy Grail, 10
Hooden Horse, 124
Howlers, 91
Hunters Moon Morris, 94
Hutton, Ronald, 84, 117,
Jennifer Gentle, 51-6, 134
John Barleycorn, 57-62, 134-5
Kerridwen, 41, 116
The King of the Faeries (tune), 144
King Orfeo, 63-70, 104, 136
Knightley, Steve, 126
Lady Margaret, 71-6, 136
The Laidly Worm, 78-9
Lammas, 62
The Lambton Worm, 77-82, 137
Lloyd, A.L., 34, 42
Maid Marian, 46, 50
Mari Lywd, 94
May Day, 44,
Merlin, 21-5, 92, 109-10
Mermaids, 27, 33-6
Midsummer, 30, 57
Moon, 55, 88, 107, 112
More, Sir Thomas, 56
Morris Dancing, 46, 49, 67, 93-4
Mumming, 44, 46
Nostrodamus, 2
Old Molly Hare (see *Faery Dance*)
Padstow May Song, 49
Pagan rites – survival of, 14-18, 30, 42, 50, 61, 67, 70, 81, 84, 94, 118
Paganism, ancient, 19, 29, 40, 117
Paganism, modern, 42, 94
Parsley Sage Rosemary & Thyme, 54
Pepys, Samuel, 59
Renaud, Jean, 33

Rickert, Edith, 16
Ritual murder, 28, 59
Robin Hood, 46, 49, 112
Sacrifice, 8, 14, 19, 28, 40, 61, 102, 111
Saint George , 44, 46, 48-9
Saint Michael, 44, 46, 48-9
Saint Stephen, 19, 39, 42
Scot, Michael, 111
Scott, Walter, 74, 76, 104, 110,
Shakespeare, William, 30, 50, 56, 68, 75-6, 86, 112, 124
Shape-shifting, 27-8, 35, 101-2, 115-17
Sharp, Cecil, 38, 58-9, 92, 115, 121
Sheebeg Sheemore, 67, 145
Silver, 25, 55, 75, 83, 88, 108
Somerset Wassail, 83-94, 138
Songs of Witchcraft and Magic, 6
Spirit Paths (see corpse roads)
Standing Stones, 8, 10, 66-7, 124
Stewart, Bob, 40, 53, 70, 116-7,
Sweet William's Ghost, 73
Taliesin, 41, 116-18
Tam Lin (tune), 142
Tam Lin, 66, 95-104, 139
Tavistock Goosey Fair, 123
The Two Magicians, 27, 113-18, 140
Thomas the Rhymer, 66, 104, 105-112, 139
Vaughan Williams, Ralph, 8, 12
Wassail Chants, 40, 90-92
Wassailing (see *Somerset Wassail*)
Waterson, Mike, 50
Wear, river (see *Lambton Worm*)
Where is Saint George?, 40, 117
White Hart 63, 69
Widdecombe Fair, 141
Widecombe-in-the-Moor, 119-126
Witchcraft, 2, 4, 34-5, 56, 80, 112, 116
Yule, 12, 18
Zennor, 35-6

www.ingramcontent.com/pod-product-compliance
Lightning Source LLC
Chambersburg PA
CBHW070807100426
42742CB00012B/2282